# CNN News English:
## Engaging College Students as Active Learners

Tsukasa Yamanaka

Rafael Roman

Chiho Toyoshima

Asahi Press

## 音声再生アプリ「リスニング・トレーナー」を使った音声ダウンロード

朝日出版社開発のアプリ、「リスニング・トレーナー（リストレ）」を使えば、教科書の音声をスマホ、タブレットに簡単にダウンロードできます。どうぞご活用ください。

### ◉ アプリ【リスニング・トレーナー】の使い方

**《アプリのダウンロード》**

App Store または Google Play から「リスニング・トレーナー」のアプリ（無料）をダウンロード

App Storeはこちら▶ 　　Google Playはこちら▶

**《アプリの使い方》**

① アプリを開き「コンテンツを追加」をタップ
② 画面上部に【15715】を入力しDoneをタップ

## 映像・音声ストリーミング配信 》》》

この教科書の映像及び音声は、右記ウェブサイトにて無料で配信しています。

　https://text.asahipress.com/free/english/

# Preface

## *Envisioning the Future of University English Education in the Age of AI*

As the spotlight intensifies on machine translation and generative AI within society, the landscape of university-level English education stands on the precipice of a profound qualitative metamorphosis in the forthcoming years. Yet, in the practical realm, few instructors possess a clear roadmap for implementing these transformative changes. For many engaged in the pedagogy of English education, it appears that the quest for answers will persist in the meantime.

The authors, much like many others, do not hold a definitive response regarding the future objectives of university-level English education. However, in this era of rapid evolution, focusing on elements that are unchanging and firmly set may offer insight into this problem. Regardless of the extent to which AI integrates into our lives, the foundational principle of human communication through language, the exchange of meanings, and the iterative process of discourse shall undeniably endure. Naturally, the realm of "others" with whom we communicate may include AI-equipped robots in the future.

Generative AI responses may propose one "possible answer," but this is by no means a definitive solution. By infusing the unique human originality inherent in each individual, expressions and communications that only a person can create will persist as objects of importance and value. Consequently, the ability to autonomously showcase and advance oneself through English becomes indispensable. Therefore, it is justifiable that university-level English education serves as the trial for nurturing, demonstrating, and honing this skill. It is with this consciousness that the authors have penned this volume.

## *Pursuing the Creation of Educational Materials that Foster Communication, Deep Contemplation, and Genuine Interest*

This volume draws inspiration from relatively recent news articles featured on CNN, striving to transcend superficial comprehension in favor of an unwavering exploration of the subjects at hand. The selection of CNN news articles as the foundation for this book stems not only from CNN's renown and linguistic sophistication but, most importantly, from the articles' reflection of real-world events. Authenticity is the quintessential pedagogical tool, and we invite you to contemplate these global issues as if they were "your own affairs," for we all coexist on this planet.

The challenges confronting our world are complex, devoid of universal and equitable solutions. Each and every one of you possesses unique insights, and this is no jest. This book adopts this perspective and poses numerous inquiries, recognizing that multiple answers may exist. It is plausible that some concepts may prove challenging to articulate fluently in English, a second language for many. Nonetheless, we encourage you to pursue the content without compromise, as your proficiency in English will assuredly progress in tandem.

We aspire for this material to kindle genuine intellectual curiosity.

On behalf of the author,
Tsukasa Yamanaka

# Chapter overview

Each unit has been divided into 8 parts which will be explained below.

## 1. Check In

Each unit begins with two question prompts. The questions are related to the topic and meant to promote discussion before the lesson activities. This section will allow you to use your current knowledge of the topic and warm-up before the lesson begins.

## 2. Listening Exercise 1: Opening paragraph

This section introduces the topic paragraph of the news article. This introduces the theme of the unit. There are two question prompts. They allow you to discuss the general idea of the news story. They also allow you to predict or imagine what information will be given in each news segment.

## 3. Listening Exercise 2: Let's listen to the full story.

This section is a listening exercise on a news story. Using the information from parts 1 and 2 should help in your preparation for this listening activity and what information the news story will give. This section includes three questions which focus on the main ideas of the news story. These questions will help you get a general understanding of the news story.

## 4. Listening Exercise 3: Comprehension

This section includes six listening comprehension questions that focus on the more detailed parts of the news stories. The questions include three true or false questions and three multiple choice questions. Many of the questions highlight important key information. These questions will help you focus on and learn the important small details the news story discusses.

## 5. Creating a Summary

This section provides two options for you to explore.

Option A allows you to focus more on organizing your information through design and writing. You can choose to create diagrams or visual aids as well as sentences to help explain the story to others.

Option B allows you to focus more on organizing your information through speaking and presenting. You can create your own speech and decide what information you will focus on to share with others.

## 6. Debate Exercise

The section focuses on debate. It provides a prompt related to the news story. The prompt will let you choose a pro side or con side to focus on. Each section includes an example argument, either pro or con, which you can use to structure your argument. Pro and Con teams are given two prompts they can explain in more detail.

In addition, there are two additional debate prompts you can use to practice creating arguments related to the topic.

## 7. Mini-Research

This section focuses on research related to the news topic. It provides five themes and you are allowed to choose one theme to focus on and research. These themes allow you to think further about the story. You can gain useful research skills and think about the topic more deeply.

This section provides two options for you to explore.

Option A allows you to focus more on your writing skills. You can choose to create an essay. This will help you to practice organizing your information into a clear essay argument. This will be useful for your writing skills.

Option B allows you to focus more on your speaking skills. You can choose to create a slide presentation. This will help you to practice organizing your information into clear slides and developing a speech to share your ideas. This will be useful in your speaking skills.

## 8. Project

This section focuses on combining all the skills and information you used for this unit. It offers two prompts which discuss the news story. These prompts are future focused meaning they do not have a fixed answer. You will need to study, research, and share your information in a clear and cohesive way.

Project prompts allow you to freely explore the topic and come to your own conclusions and opinions.

# Usage Guidelines

This textbook is crafted to facilitate English language learning for individuals of varying proficiency levels and across diverse learning contexts. We encourage you to harness its interactive features to enhance your English skills effectively. There are multiple ways to utilize it: you can choose from the activities outlined below or even incorporate your own original activities into the book.

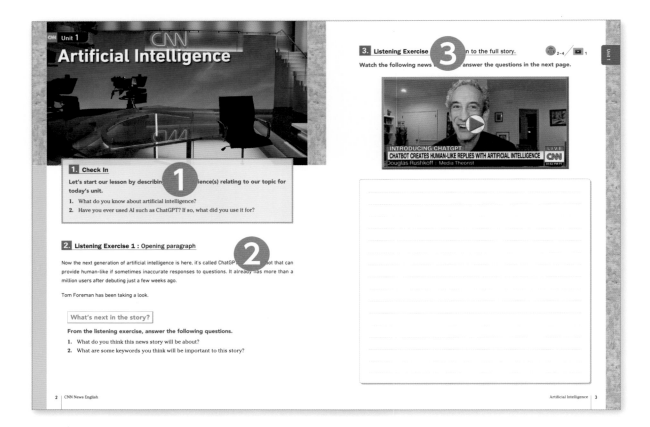

## ① Check In

This section focuses on casual conversation, often referred to as "small talk." Some topics may be familiar to you, while others might be new. You can engage with your fellow students, discussing what you know and discuss the subjects covered in this Unit.

## ② Listening Exercise 1

Media reports in Japan and worldwide typically follow a structure called the "inverted triangle." This means that the most important information is presented at the beginning, followed by additional details later on. While media reports may need to be adjusted in length depending on available space, these edits usually occur towards the end. The opening paragraphs of these reports are crucial as they contain essential information vital to the entire story. Paying extra attention to these initial paragraphs is advisable as they provide valuable insights into the overall content of the report.

1.  **What is the purpose of the news story?**

    a.  To promote the use of AI in various artistic fields such as music or paintings
    b.  To warn people about the potential dangers to the job market due to AI
    c.  To demonstrate how self-driving cars work with AI on the road
    d.  To inform the audience about the capabilities and impact of ChatGPT

2.  **The word "humanoid" is in the news story to describe ChatGPT. Which option has the closest meaning:**

    a.  A skilled novelist
    b.  Behavior similar to a computer
    c.  Human-like behavior
    d.  A robot-like entity

3.  **From the news story, what problems does ChatGPT say it has?**

    a.  It uses imaginary citations and creates fake information.
    b.  It admits to making mistakes and sometimes getting things wrong.
    c.  It writes in a repetitive way which is easy to identify.
    d.  It is limited in its knowledge so it requires more data.

---

**4. Listening Exercise 3: Comprehension**

**4**

Using the information you learned in the news story, select the best answer for each question.

1.  **According to the news report, ChatGPT has had more than a million users since it started.**

    a.  True
    b.  False

2.  **According to the news report, the professor interviewed, Douglas Rushkoff, is not impressed with ChatGPT's writings.**

    a.  True
    b.  False

3.  **According to the news report, ChatGPT's knowledge is limited to only the year 2021.**

    a.  True
    b.  False

4.  **In the news report, what are some potential concerns brought up by Professor Rushkoff?**

    a.  It will help with the production of new jobs and careers.
    b.  It will help people save time and resources necessary to create something.
    c.  It will not be able to improve quickly due to the large number of users.
    d.  It will hurt human connections and impact the job market.

5.  **According to the news report, how does ChatGPT create material?**

    a.  It scans the internet to look for the most accurate information.
    b.  It learns from each human interaction to grow and develop.
    c.  It works with other AI programs to share information and generate information.
    d.  It is programmed in advance with a set of specific prompts.

6.  **According to the news story, what is the future of ChatGPT?**

    a.  ChatGPT will encourage other companies to create AI programs to compete.
    b.  ChatGPT will become more mainstream and be life-changing as it improves.
    c.  ChatGPT will become dangerous and require governmental intervention.
    d.  ChatGPT will replace human interactions and be adopted by major companies.

## ③ Listening Exercise 2

In this listening exercise, you will watch an actual CNN news clip to grasp the main points of the story. This news has been broadcast worldwide in the past, allowing people worldwide to stay informed. Try to engage with it not only as a learner, but as a global citizen. We encourage you to feel connected to the story.

## ④ Listening Exercise 3

This section assesses the accuracy of your understanding of the news content. You can use this as a simple test or engage in detailed analysis for each option to ensure thorough comprehension. Consider this as an opportunity to go into the content by understanding why certain options are correct, as well as why others are incorrect. You could also rephrase the options to create a unique and correct answer.

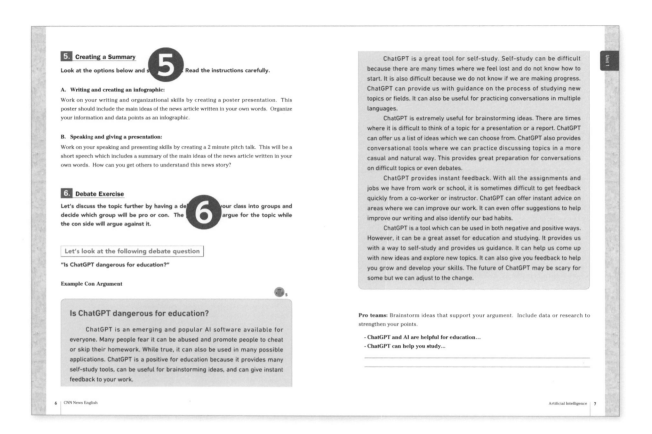

# ⑤ Creating a Summary

In this section, rather than using receptive skills (listening, reading), you'll learn how to comprehend news articles through productive skills (speaking, writing). Two specific activities are provided: A. Written communication using an infographic and B. Verbal communication using a presentation. Both are essential skills to develop, so choose the one you find more challenging or alternate between them. The writing activity using infographics in A aims to create a visually appealing poster with effective verbal explanations. The speaking activity in B using a presentation aims to develop a student's voice as they organize their ideas into a meaningful speech which will improve their communicative skills. It might be challenging initially, but you will improve with practice.

# ⑥ Debate Exercise

Debates are not solely about winning or losing but rather a method to identify opposing viewpoints and essential points of contention. Engaging in a confrontational manner reveals perspectives from different angles. Regardless of your debating experience or proficiency, the primary goal isn't winning but gaining valuable experience in deepening your debates using English. This textbook provides numerous suggestions for conducting debates. Utilize them as needed to enhance your debating skills.

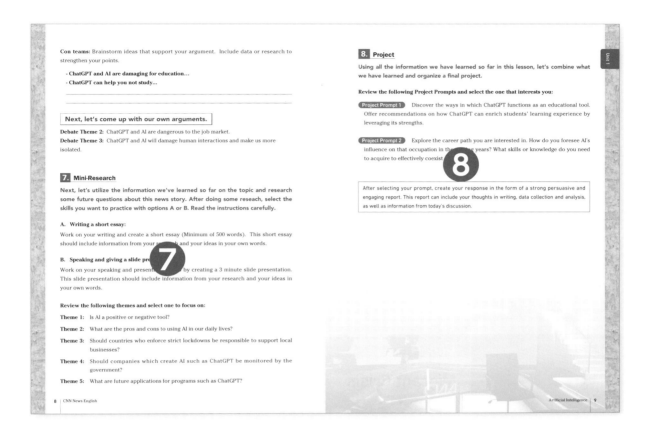

## ⑦ Mini-Research

We have presented five "themes" to explore the Unit's topic extensively and from various perspectives. Some of these questions are highly controversial and can be discussed deeply. They have been thoughtfully chosen for your consideration. You can work on all of them or focus on those of particular interest. We have specified two presentation modes: written and spoken. Understand their characteristics and thoroughly explore the content. The key is not only expressing yourself in English but also producing outstanding research results.

## ⑧ Project

As the Unit's culmination, we offer two unique projects that go beyond the Unit's research activities and involve proposing specific actions and solutions. The keywords here are originality and evidence. Be innovative, develop distinctive projects from perspectives that others haven't explored, and collect sufficient evidence to persuade your audience. It's ideal if you can initiate a project based on your interests and passions while incorporating insights from Unit discussions. You have the option to work individually or collaborate in groups.

# CONTENTS

Unit 1
Artificial Intelligence ················································· 2

Unit 2
Student Loan Forgiveness ······································· 10

Unit 3
Augmented Reality ················································· 18

Unit 4
Migrant Crisis ······················································· 26

Unit 5
Cryptocurrency Mining ··········································· 34

Unit 6
Population Decline ················································· 42

Unit 7
Global Warming ····················································· 50

Unit 8
Shark Tourism ······················································· 58

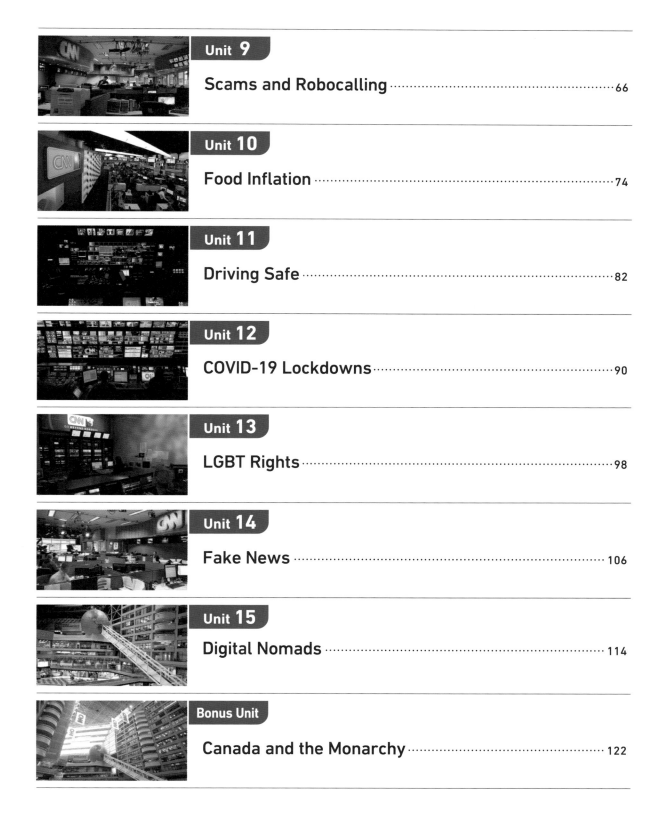

Unit 9

Scams and Robocalling ···························································· 66

Unit 10

Food Inflation ········································································· 74

Unit 11

Driving Safe ············································································ 82

Unit 12

COVID-19 Lockdowns ······························································· 90

Unit 13

LGBT Rights ············································································ 98

Unit 14

Fake News ·············································································· 106

Unit 15

Digital Nomads ········································································ 114

Bonus Unit

Canada and the Monarchy ························································ 122

# Artificial Intelligence

## 1. Check In

Let's start our lesson by describing your experience(s) relating to our topic for today's unit.

1. What do you know about artificial intelligence?
2. Have you ever used AI such as ChatGPT? If so, what did you use it for?

## 2. Listening Exercise 1 : Opening paragraph

Now the next generation of artificial intelligence is here, it's called ChatGPT. It is a chatbot that can provide human-like if sometimes inaccurate responses to questions. It already has more than a million users after debuting just a few weeks ago.

Tom Foreman has been taking a look.

### What's next in the story?

From the listening exercise, answer the following questions.

1. What do you think this news story will be about?
2. What are some keywords you think will be important to this story?

## 3. Listening Exercise 2: Let's listen to the full story.

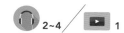 2~4 / 1

**Watch the following news video and answer the questions in the next page.**

1. **What is the purpose of the news story?**

   a. To promote the use of AI in various artistic fields such as music or paintings

   b. To warn people about the potential dangers to the job market due to AI

   c. To demonstrate how self-driving cars work with AI on the road

   d. To inform the audience about the capabilities and impact of ChatGPT

2. **The word "humanoid" is in the news story to describe ChatGPT. Which option has the closest meaning:**

   a. A skilled novelist

   b. Behavior similar to a computer

   c. Human-like behavior

   d. A robot-like entity

3. **From the news story, what problems does ChatGPT say it has?**

   a. It uses imaginary citations and creates fake information.

   b. It admits to making mistakes and sometimes getting things wrong.

   c. It writes in a repetitive way which is easy to identify.

   d. It is limited in its knowledge so it requires more data.

## 4. Listening Exercise 3: Comprehension

Using the information you learned in the news story, select the best answer for each question.

1. According to the news report, ChatGPT has had more than a million users since it started.

   a. True
   b. False

2. According to the news report, the professor interviewed, Douglas Rushkoff, is not impressed with ChatGPT's writings.

   a. True
   b. False

3. According to the news report, ChatGPT's knowledge is limited to only the year 2021.

   a. True
   b. False

4. In the news report, what are some potential concerns brought up by Professor Rushkoff?

   a. It will help with the production of new jobs and careers.
   b. It will help people save time and resources necessary to create something.
   c. It will not be able to improve quickly due to the large number of users.
   d. It will hurt human connections and impact the job market.

5. According to the news report, how does ChatGPT create material?

   a. It scans the internet to look for the most accurate information.
   b. It learns from each human interaction to grow and develop.
   c. It works with other AI programs to share information and generate information.
   d. It is programmed in advance with a set of specific prompts.

6. According to the news story, what is the future of ChatGPT?

   a. ChatGPT will encourage other companies to create AI programs to compete.
   b. ChatGPT will become more mainstream and be life-changing as it improves.
   c. ChatGPT will become dangerous and require governmental intervention.
   d. ChatGPT will replace human interactions and be adopted by major companies.

## 5. Creating a Summary

**Look at the options below and select A or B. Read the instructions carefully.**

**A. Writing and creating an infographic:**

Work on your writing and organizational skills by creating a poster presentation. This poster should include the main ideas of the news article written in your own words. Organize your information and data points as an infographic.

**B. Speaking and giving a presentation:**

Work on your speaking and presenting skills by creating a 2 minute pitch talk. This will be a short speech which includes a summary of the main ideas of the news article written in your own words. How can you get others to understand this news story?

## 6. Debate Exercise

**Let's discuss the topic further by having a debate. Split your class into groups and decide which group will be pro or con. The pro side will argue for the topic while the con side will argue against it.**

Let's look at the following debate question

**"Is ChatGPT dangerous for education?"**

**Example Con Argument**

 5

### Is ChatGPT dangerous for education?

ChatGPT is an emerging and popular AI software available for everyone. Many people fear it can be abused and promote people to cheat or skip their homework. While true, it can also be used in many possible applications. ChatGPT is a positive for education because it provides many self-study tools, can be useful for brainstorming ideas, and can give instant feedback to your work.

ChatGPT is a great tool for self-study. Self-study can be difficult because there are many times where we feel lost and do not know how to start. It is also difficult because we do not know if we are making progress. ChatGPT can provide us with guidance on the process of studying new topics or fields. It can also be useful for practicing conversations in multiple languages.

ChatGPT is extremely useful for brainstorming ideas. There are times where it is difficult to think of a topic for a presentation or a report. ChatGPT can offer us a list of ideas which we can choose from. ChatGPT also provides conversational tools where we can practice discussing topics in a more casual and natural way. This provides great preparation for conversations on difficult topics or even debates.

ChatGPT provides instant feedback. With all the assignments and jobs we have from work or school, it is sometimes difficult to get feedback quickly from a co-worker or instructor. ChatGPT can offer instant advice on areas where we can improve our work. It can even offer suggestions to help improve our writing and also identify our bad habits.

ChatGPT is a tool which can be used in both negative and positive ways. However, it can be a great asset for education and studying. It provides us with a way to self-study and provides us guidance. It can help us come up with new ideas and explore new topics. It can also give you feedback to help you grow and develop your skills. The future of ChatGPT may be scary for some but we can adjust to the change.

**Pro teams:** Brainstorm ideas that support your argument. Include data or research to strengthen your points.

- **ChatGPT and AI are helpful for education…**
- **ChatGPT can help you study…**

_____

_____

**Con teams:** Brainstorm ideas that support your argument.  Include data or research to strengthen your points.

- **ChatGPT and AI are damaging for education...**
- **ChatGPT can help you not study...**

_____

_____

> ## Next, let's come up with our own arguments.

**Debate Theme 2:**  ChatGPT and AI are dangerous to the job market.

**Debate Theme 3:**  ChatGPT and AI will damage human interactions and make us more isolated.


## 7. Mini-Research

Next, let's utilize the information we've learned so far on the topic and research some future questions about this news story. After doing some reseach, select the skills you want to practice with options A or B. Read the instructions carefully.

### A.  Writing a short essay:

Work on your writing and create a short essay (Minimum of 500 words).  This short essay should include information from your research and your ideas in your own words.

### B.  Speaking and giving a slide presentation:

Work on your speaking and presentation skills by creating a 3 minute slide presentation. This slide presentation should include information from your research and your ideas in your own words.

**Review the following themes and select one to focus on:**

**Theme 1:**   Is AI a positive or negative tool?

**Theme 2:**   What are the pros and cons to using AI in our daily lives?

**Theme 3:**   Should countries who enforce strict lockdowns be responsible to support local businesses?

**Theme 4:**   Should companies which create AI such as ChatGPT be monitored by the government?

**Theme 5:**   What are future applications for programs such as ChatGPT?

## 8. Project

Using all the information we have learned so far in this lesson, let's combine what we have learned and organize a final project.

**Review the following Project Prompts and select the one that interests you:**

**Project Prompt 1**    Discover the ways in which ChatGPT functions as an educational tool. Offer recommendations on how ChatGPT can enrich students' learning experience by leveraging its strengths.

**Project Prompt 2**    Explore the career path you are interested in. How do you foresee AI's influence on that occupation in the coming years? What skills or knowledge do you need to acquire to effectively coexist with AI?

After selecting your prompt, create your response in the form of a strong persuasive and engaging report. This report can include your thoughts in writing, data collection and analysis, as well as information from today's discussion.

# Student Loan Forgiveness

## 1. Check In

**Let's start our lesson by describing your experience(s) relating to our topic for today's unit.**

1. Have you ever had to ask for money from your friend or parents? If so, what for?
2. Should university education be available for free to all people who complete high school?

## 2. Listening Exercise 1: Opening paragraph

We're going to move now on to another major story though out of Washington. There are still a lot of unanswered questions about President Biden's newly announced student loan forgiveness plan. Like when borrowers will start to see that relief and how the country plans to pay for it as well.

CNN's Brian Todd is taking a closer look at those details.

### What's next in the story?

**From the listening exercise, answer the following questions.**

1. What do you think this news story will be about?
2. What are some keywords you think will be important to this story?

## 3. Listening Exercise 2: Let's listen to the full story.

**Watch the following news video and answer the questions in the next page.**

1. **What is the purpose of the news story?**

   a. To show the pros and cons of going to university

   b. To talk about problems with increasing university tuition and fees

   c. To discuss a conversational program which would forgive student loans

   d. To point out the unfairness of forgiving student loans

2. **The phrase "footing the bill" is used by Brian Todd discussing the critics' perspectives. Which option has the closest meaning:**

   a. Refusing to pay the cost of something

   b. Splitting the cost of something in half

   c. Collecting donations to pay the cost of something

   d. Paying the entire cost of something

3. **From the news story, what are Pell Grants?**

   a. Pell Grants are students struggling to pay their university tuition.

   b. Pell Grants help families struggling with financial support.

   c. They are people who join the military to get higher education.

   d. They are people who took a loan but did not graduate from university.

## 4. Listening Exercise 3: Comprehension

Using the information you learned in the news story, select the best answer for each question.

1. According to the news report, student loan debt is one of the main influences on household debt.

    a. True

    b. False

2. According to the news report, President Biden's new plan makes universities free for students.

    a. True

    b. False

3. According to the news report, President Biden's plan will help a majority of loan borrowers.

    a. True

    b. False

4. Who does the current plan for student loan forgiveness not support?

    a. Students who get scholarships for university tuition.

    b. Students who get private loans for their university tuition.

    c. Students who go to more expensive private universities.

    d. Students who took federal loans for university tuition.

5. What are the opinions of critics against this program?

    a. They worry that too many students will apply for this program.

    b. They are upset it only applies to a small amount of a student loan.

    c. They are upset that it only applies to people who finish their university degrees.

    d. They find the situation unfair, especially for people who find other means of going to university.

6. What does Michelle Singletary think is the true reason for this debt problem?

    a. Inflation has caused the price of daily goods to go up a significant amount.

    b. Higher education tuition has increased an unreasonable amount.

    c. University loans are harder for students to get.

    d. Many people do not see priority in getting a university degree.

## 5. Creating a Summary

**Look at the options below and select A or B. Read the instructions carefully.**

### A. Writing and creating an infographic:

Work on your writing and organizational skills by creating a poster presentation. This poster should include the main ideas of the news article written in your own words. Organize your information and data points as an infographic.

### B. Speaking and giving a presentation:

Work on your speaking and presenting skills by creating a 2 minute pitch talk. This will be a short speech which includes a summary of the main ideas of the news article written in your own words. How can you get others to understand this news story?

## 6. Debate Exercise

Let's discuss the topic further by having a debate. Split your class into groups and decide which group will be pro or con. The pro side will argue for the topic while the con side will argue against it.

Let's look at the following debate question

"Should student loans be forgiven?"

**Example Con Argument**

### Should student loans be forgiven?

Student loans should not be forgiven. Students apply for loans to support their interests. It is their choice to take a loan or not. Students should not be forgiven the loans because it will be too costly, demotivate students, and create resentment with older generations.

Student loans are too expensive to forgive. Higher education requires a lot of money for experts in specialized fields as well as advanced research. Educational equipment is also expensive as more and more schools try to use advanced equipment. Forgiving loans will cause a decrease in university income.

Forgiving student loans will demotivate students from focusing on their studies. With free or cheaper education, students will take classes less seriously. Many may drop their classes and try to apply to various different programs. This will decrease the quality of students as well as successful graduates.

This program will create anger with older generations. It is unfair for people who worked hard and paid for their university studies to now see students do not need to do the same. This will create anger between these two groups. Everyone must pay their fair share.

To summarize, forgiving student loans will be expensive, create laziness, and cause annoyance with people. Forgiving loans will cost the government a lot of money. This 'free' money will also demotivate students, allowing them to come and go as they please without penalty. Finally this program will cause distance between generations.

**Pro teams:** Brainstorm ideas that support your argument. Include data or research to strengthen your points.

**– Students can avoid student loan debt…**
**– Universities can attract a wider variety of students…**

_____

_____


**Con teams:** Brainstorm ideas that support your argument. Include data or research to strengthen your points.

**– This program is unfair…**
**– The program does not address the real problem…**

_____

_____

## Next, let's come up with our own arguments.

**Debate theme 2:** Universities should be free for all students seeking higher education.

**Debate theme 3:** Student loan forgiveness is unfair and will hurt student motivation.


## 7. Mini-Research

**Next, let's utilize the information we've learned so far on the topic and research some future questions about this news story. After doing some reseach, select the skills you want to practice with options A or B. Read the instructions carefully.**

### A. Writing a short essay:

Work on your writing and create a short essay (Minimum of 500 words). This short essay should include information from your research and your ideas in your own words.


### B. Speaking and giving a slide presentation:

Work on your speaking and presentation skills by creating a 3 minute slide presentation. This slide presentation should include information from your research and your ideas in your own words.


**Review the following themes and select one to focus on:**

**Theme 1:** Why is student loan forgiveness a hot topic right now?

**Theme 2:** Are universities charging too much for higher education?

**Theme 3:** As critics say, is it fair to give newer generations support that they themselves didn't receive?

**Theme 4:** Should the student loan forgiveness plan be decreased or increased in scope?

**Theme 5:** Should free universities be introduced as an option for students?

## 8. Project

Using all the information we have learned so far in this lesson, let's combine what we have learned and organize a final project.

**Review the following Project Prompts and select the one that interests you:**

**Project Prompt 1**    What qualities and characteristics define an ideal university? Provide a specific proposal on how to create an ideal university that will attract prospective applicants.

**Project Prompt 2**    In some countries, university tuition is offered at no cost, even for international students. Examine the given instances and contemplate how Japan's future higher education policy could be influenced by the ideas and context they represent.

---

After selecting your prompt, create your response in the form of a strong persuasive and engaging report. This report can include your thoughts in writing, data collection and analysis, as well as information from today's discussion.

# Augmented Reality

**CNN** **Unit 3**

## 1. Check In

Let's start our lesson by describing your experience(s) relating to our topic for today's unit.

1. Discuss some ways you use technology, such as your smartphone, to improve your daily life.
2. What are some ways technology supports people with special health conditions?

## 2. Listening Exercise 1: Opening paragraph

**KINKADE**: Welcome back. A new kind of smart glasses may soon change the way deaf people communicate. They allow users to actually read conversations, kind of like watching a subtitled foreign film.

CNN's Michael Holmes reports.

> What's next in the story?

**From the listening exercise, answer the following questions.**

1. What do you think this news story will be about?
2. What are some keywords you think will be important to this story?

**3.** **Listening Exercise 2:** Let's listen to the full story.  10~12 / 3

Watch the following news video and answer the questions in the next page.

AMAZING TECH
"SMART GLASSES" ADD SUBTITLES TO REAL-TIME CONVERSATIONS
LIVE
CNN
8:53 AM GMT

1. **What is the purpose of the news story?**

   a. To introduce how people with disabilities live their day-to-day lives.

   b. To explain new technology which can improve a person's vision.

   c. To demonstrate a new product supporting people with disabilities.

   d. To showcase a new company XRAI Glass and their many products.

2. **The word "epiphany" is used by CEO Dan Scarfe. Which option has the closest in meaning to:**

   a. A moment of confusion

   b. A moment of inspiration

   c. An emotional moment

   d. A difficult moment to process

3. **From the news story, how does this product work?**

   a. It uses AI such as Alexa or Siri to help answer questions and offer advice.

   b. It listens, transcribes, and displays text to the user in real time.

   c. It translates languages into English to help people communicate.

   d. It converts sound vibrations which can be felt and understood by the user.

## 4. Listening Exercise 3: Comprehension

Using the information you learned in the news story, select the best answer for each question.

1. According to the news report, this new technology is supporting people with visual impairments.

   a. True
   b. False

2. According to the news report, this technology will focus on helping the elderly.

   a. True
   b. False

3. According to the news report, this new technology will be used to help people of different countries communicate.

   a. True
   b. False

4. What information does the creator Dan Scarfe offer on why he created this product?

   a. To help a family member avoid isolation
   b. To use his engineering knowledge to create something new
   c. To help people enjoy movies with subtitles
   d. To help people with hearing impairments have a better quality of life

5. What is Josh Feldman's opinion on the product?

   a. He thinks this will promote more companies to create products for the disabled.
   b. He thinks the product uses a lot of power and will need frequent recharging.
   c. He thinks it will help people with hearing disabilities enjoy movie subtitles.
   d. He thinks it will improve communication with people with hearing disabilities.

6. The news story mentions that his product is still in "beta". Which option has the closest meaning?

   a. This product is the second version and less expensive than the original.
   b. This product will be used in various situations such as cross cultural communication.
   c. This product is still under development and being improved on.
   d. This product will have a limited release and be difficult to purchase.

## 5. Creating a Summary

**Look at the options below and select A or B. Read the instructions carefully.**

**A. Writing and creating an infographic:**

Work on your writing and organizational skills by creating a poster presentation. This poster should include the main ideas of the news article written in your own words. Organize your information and data points as an infographic.

**B. Speaking and giving a presentation:**

Work on your speaking and presenting skills by creating a 2 minute pitch talk. This will be a short speech which includes a summary of the main ideas of the news article written in your own words. How can you get others to understand this news story?

## 6. Debate Exercise

**Let's discuss the topic further by having a debate. Split your class into groups and decide which group will be pro or con. The pro side will argue for the topic while the con side will argue against it.**

Let's look at the following debate question

**"Will this new product change how people communicate?"**

**Example Con Argument**

 13

### Will this new product change how people communicate?

New products will always be created but many do not last. This product is a specialized product which will help people with hearing impairments. However, this product will not change how people communicate because it has a limited market, requires too much energy, and will interrupt communication.

This product helps a few groups of people. This means it cannot be mass produced or sold to many people. This will make it expensive since it is mainly for the hearing impaired. Other products will be much cheaper and provide similar results.

This product requires too much power. It will need a large physical battery to power all day but also need to use a lot of our 'mental' battery. It will require us to focus and read a lot of information quickly. This can be quite tiring for us to do all day.

Lastly, this will decrease the quality of our conversations or communications. Of course, people with hearing impairments will benefit but as the article mentioned the company is also planning translation services. This means instead of hearing a translator we will be trying to read translations of what people say which could lead to misunderstandings.

In conclusion, this product, while good for some, will not help most people. It will be costly and require a lot of care and attention. This can be in the form of recharging the device or resting our eyes and minds throughout the day. It will also cause our communication to be less smooth and natural with people staring at a screen instead of each other.

**Pro teams:** Brainstorm ideas that support your argument. Include data or research to strengthen your points.

**– This product will improve communication…**
**– Cross cultural communication will improve…**

_____

_____

**Con teams:** Brainstorm ideas that support your argument. Include data or research to strengthen your points.

**– This product will hurt communication…**
**– Cross cultural communication will decline…**

_____

_____

## Next, let's come up with our own arguments.

**Debate Theme 2:** XRAI's product will change communication for all people, not only the hearing impaired.

**Debate theme 3:** Technology which promotes communication will become more common in the future.

## 7. Mini-Research

**Next, let's utilize the information we've learned so far on the topic and research some future questions about this news story. After doing some reseach, select the skills you want to practice with options A or B. Read the instructions carefully.**

### A. Writing a short essay:

Work on your writing and create a short essay (Minimum of 500 words). This short essay should include information from your research and your ideas in your own words.

### B. Speaking and giving a slide presentation:

Work on your speaking and presentation skills by creating a 3 minute slide presentation. This slide presentation should include information from your research and your ideas in your own words.

**Review the following themes and select one to focus on:**

**Theme 1:** What are some other products that are currently available to help people with disabilities?

**Theme 2:** What limitations will the product have in the real world?

**Theme 3:** As smart devices become more popular, will more companies create tools for people with disabilities?

**Theme 4:** Does technology improve communication or hurt it?

**Theme 5:** How else do you think people could use this product?

## 8. Project

**Using all the information we have learned so far in this lesson, let's combine what we have learned and organize a final project.**

**Review the following Project Prompts and select the one that interests you:**

**Project Prompt 1**    Present ideas or policies for new products, such as smart glasses, that can enhance the lives of people with disabilities.

**Project Prompt 2**    Identify specific challenges faced by individuals with impairments in their daily lives and suggest solutions that society should address to ease these difficulties.

After selecting your prompt, create your response in the form of a strong persuasive and engaging report. This report can include your thoughts in writing, data collection and analysis, as well as information from today's discussion.

# Migrant Crisis

**CNN**

## 1. Check In

**Let's start our lesson by describing your experience(s) relating to our topic for today's unit.**

1. Should more countries open their borders to allow people from overseas to come to live?
2. How much support should a country provide people from overseas?

## 2. Listening Exercise 1: Opening paragraph

Now New York City is opening a new facility today to serve 500 asylum seekers. The tent center on Randall's Island cost $325,000 to set up. But the city is still calculating the day-to-day operating costs. While some New Yorkers are not happy about the influx of migrants, others are doing what they can to help.

CNN's Miguel Marquez has the story.

> **What's next in the story?**

**From the listening exercise, answer the following questions.**

1. What do you think this news story will be about?
2. What are some keywords you think will be important to this story?

## 3. Listening Exercise 2: Let's listen to the full story.

14~16 / ▶ 4

**Watch the following news video and answer the questions in the next page.**

1. **What is the purpose of the news story?**

   a. To discuss the current crisis New York is facing with a surge of incoming migrants

   b. To explain how people are helping others by supporting them financially and with donations

   c. To understand why people are immigrating to the United States in large numbers

   d. To show the generosity of some business owners like Verde's pizza shop

2. **The phrase "asylum-seeker" is used in the news story. Which option has the closest in meaning to:**

   a. Someone looking for higher education in a new country

   b. Someone who needs to go to the hospital

   c. Someone trying to escape their current country

   d. Someone who is looking for temporary work in a new country

3. **From the news story, why is this migrant crisis so challenging for New York?**

   a. New York tourists have booked most of the rooms in the hotels.

   b. New York locals are not happy with the incoming migrants.

   c. Many migrants are coming with no local connection or support.

   d. Many migrants lack skills for getting a job.

## 4. Listening Exercise 3: Comprehension

Using the information you learned in the news story, select the best answer for each question.

1. According to the news reports, New Yorkers have mixed feelings on the incoming migrants.

   a. True

   b. False

2. According to the news report, a majority of the migrants are coming from South America.

   a. True

   b. False

3. According to the news report, less than 5,000 children will enter the New York school system.

   a. True

   b. False

4. In the news story, the phrase "pitching in" is used by Miguel Martez. Which of these options is the closest in meaning?

   a. Throwing something as hard as you can

   b. Supporting something physically or financially

   c. Advertising something to get as many donations as possible

   d. Offering cheap menu options to customers

5. How does religion factor into the news story and the migrant crisis?

   a. People are very generous and welcoming of the migrants.

   b. People are very angry and against the welcoming of the migrants.

   c. Religious differences have divided people and made them not work well together.

   d. Religious attitudes had no effect on the migrant crisis.

6. In the news story, how much does the mayor estimate the cost will be in just one year?

   a. Less than one million

   b. One million

   c. Half a billion

   d. One billion

## 5. Creating a Summary

**Look at the options below and select A or B. Read the instructions carefully.**

**A. Writing and creating an infographic:**

Work on your writing and organizational skills by creating a poster presentation. This poster should include the main ideas of the news article written in your own words. Organize your information and data points as an infographic.

**B. Speaking and giving a presentation:**

Work on your speaking and presenting skills by creating a 2 minute pitch talk. This will be a short speech which includes a summary of the main ideas of the news article written in your own words. How can you get others to understand this news story?

## 6. Debate Exercise

**Let's discuss the topic further by having a debate. Split your class into groups and decide which group will be pro or con. The pro side will argue for the topic while the con side will argue against it.**

> **Let's look at the following debate question**

**"Should more countries open their borders and accept asylum seekers?"**

**Example Con Argument**

 17

### Should more countries open their borders and accept asylum seekers?

Asylum seekers are a very difficult challenge for many countries. Taking care of them requires a lot of effort and coordination. I think countries should not open their borders to asylum seekers because they require a lot of money, space, and time to adjust to the local culture.

Asylum seekers require a lot of money. Many of them are coming from countries with very little resources and so they require a lot of support. This comes in the form of shelter, food, clothing, as well as education. Many migrants cannot speak the local language so education will need more funding.

Asylum seekers also need places to stay. Finding housing for large families will be difficult for many areas. Housing is more than just a room. It also includes electricity, water, and other basic needs. This can be incredibly difficult for cities or governments to arrange.

Adjusting to a new culture also takes a lot of time and effort. Asylum seekers are fleeing or running away from difficult situations. Many have trauma which will make it difficult for them to adjust socially. Language will also be a barrier and it will take time to get them to understand their new homes.

Due to these reasons, countries should not open their borders to asylum seekers. Although we should help people, we have to consider the responsibilities involved in taking care of these people properly. This includes housing, getting them jobs, as well as adjusting them to a new environment. These situations need to be considered deeply before accepting them into a new country.

**Pro teams:** Brainstorm ideas that support your argument. Include data or research to strengthen your points.

**– Countries should accept asylum seekers because...**
**– Asylum seekers are great additions to cities because...**

_____

_____

**Con teams:** Brainstorm ideas that support your argument. Include data or research to strengthen your points.

**– Countries should not accept asylum seekers because...**
**– Asylum seekers can cause problems such as...**

_____

_____

## Next, let's come up with our own arguments.

**Debate Theme 2:** Asylum seekers should be provided with their own areas to live in and develop.

**Debate Theme 3:** Politicians should focus more on international problems to avoid these issues before they happen.

## 7. Mini-Research

**Next, let's utilize the information we've learned so far on the topic and research some future questions about this news story. After doing some reseach, select the skills you want to practice with options A or B. Read the instructions carefully.**

### A. Writing a short essay:

Work on your writing and create a short essay (Minimum of 500 words). This short essay should include information from your research and your ideas in your own words.

### B. Speaking and giving a slide presentation:

Work on your speaking and presentation skills by creating a 3 minute slide presentation. This slide presentation should include information from your research and your ideas in your own words.

**Review the following themes and select one to focus on:**

**Theme 1:** Asylum seekers are a benefit to society over time.

**Theme 2:** Asylum seekers cause tension and break down local communities.

**Theme 3:** More countries should have special measures to provide for asylum seekers.

**Theme 4:** Asylum seeking will increase in the future due to various conflicts.

**Theme 5:** Asylum seeking will decrease in the future due to globalization.

## 8. Project

**Using all the information we have learned so far in this lesson, let's combine what we have learned and organize a final project.**

**Review the following Project Prompts and select the one that interests you:**

**Project Prompt 1**   Some argue that one of the primary motivations behind the United Kingdom's decision to leave the EU was related to their refugee policies. As a pragmatic approach, what steps could Japan consider exploring to potentially enhance their acceptance of refugees in the future?

**Project Prompt 2**   There is a viewpoint that Japan could enhance its international reputation by welcoming refugees and allowing them into the country. Share your perspective on this issue, expressing whether you are in favor or against it, and provide a rationale for your stance.

After selecting your prompt, create your response in the form of a strong persuasive and engaging report. This report can include your thoughts in writing, data collection and analysis, as well as information from today's discussion.

# Cryptocurrency Mining

## 1. Check In

**Let's start our lesson by describing your experience(s) relating to our topic for today's unit.**

1. Have you ever made a digital purchase? If so, what did you buy?
2. Do you use more physical or digital money?

## 2. Listening Exercise 1: Opening paragraph

**NEWTON**: Now the crypto exchange BitFront is the industry's latest casualty. The company said it's shutting down because of the challenges in the crypto world but maintain the decision was not driven by the collapse of FTX which has shaken confidence in digital currencies worldwide.

Even so, some major crypto assets, you can see there, jumped on Tuesday. That means though that despite the turmoil, crypto mining in fact is still a hot prospect as Anna Stewart shows us in this report.

### What's next in the story?

**From the listening exercise, answer the following questions.**

1. What do you think this news story will be about?
2. What are some keywords you think will be important to this story?

## 3. Listening Exercise 2: Let's listen to the full story.

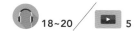

Watch the following news video and answer the questions in the next page.

1. **What is the purpose of the news story?**

   a. To discuss the crypto exchange BitFront and its sudden closing

   b. To introduce the dangers of cryptocurrency to the environment

   c. To explain how some countries are creating solutions involving cryptocurrency

   d. To present a new way to farm by using greenhouses in Sweden

2. **The word "abundant" is used in the news story. Which option has the closest in meaning to:**

   a. Something limited

   b. Something scarce

   c. Something plentiful

   d. Something hidden

3. **From the news story, how is one crypto mining company trying to help the environment?**

   a. They are using the excess heat output of crypto mining to start a greenhouse.

   b. They are donating money they collect from crypto mining to environmental programs.

   c. They are trying to reduce the amount of energy used in crypto mining by using natural energy.

   d. They are using excess heat to warm buildings in cold climate areas.

## 4. Listening Exercise 3: Comprehension

Using the information you learned in the news story, select the best answer for each question.

1. According to the news report, crypto mining involves many computers and resembles a quiet office without workers.

   a. True
   b. False

2. According to the news report, the town of Boden uses solar energy to help power the crypto mining company.

   a . True
   b. False

3. According to the news report, a company called Alquira will try to grow tomatoes and cucumbers year round.

   a. True
   b. False

4. In the news report, what was the major reason for creating this business in northern Sweden?

   a. There are many programmers from Sweden who are looking for work.
   b. There are a lot of cheap and renewable energy sources.
   c. The Swedish government has offered some incentives for new businesses.
   d. The area is becoming a new technological hotspot for new companies.

5. According to the news report, why was the Boden community inviting businesses to their area?

   a. To help populate their cities which were mainly empty
   b. To create more job opportunities for local citizens
   c. To increase the amount of cryptocurrencies in the market
   d. To utilize natural energy sources which were not being used

6. In the news story, Johanna Thornblad mentions her company "decided to bet" on the northern area. Which of these options is the closest in meaning?

   a. Avoided at first but ultimately agree to
   b. Gambled their success on
   c. Took a chance on something
   d. Chose because it was popular

## 5. Creating a Summary

**Look at the options below and select A or B. Read the instructions carefully.**

**A. Writing and creating an infographic:**

Work on your writing and organizational skills by creating a poster presentation. This poster should include the main ideas of the news article written in your own words. Organize your information and data points as an infographic.

**B. Speaking and giving a presentation:**

Work on your speaking and presenting skills by creating a 2 minute pitch talk. This will be a short speech which includes a summary of the main ideas of the news article written in your own words. How can you get others to understand this news story?

## 6. Debate Exercise

Let's discuss the topic further by having a debate. Split your class into groups and decide which group will be pro or con. The pro side will argue for the topic while the con side will argue against it.

Let's look at the following debate question

"Will crypto mining become more popular in the future?"

**Example Pro Argument**

 21

### Will crypto mining become more popular in the future?

As technology develops so does its application. This means how we use technology will change over time. Crypto mining is currently done by special computer centers but as we develop, it will become more commonplace. Crypto mining will become popular due to technological advancements, the potential for user profits, and its emergence as a global currency.

Crypto mining technology will improve in the future and this will make it more popular with users. At the moment, huge spaces and equipment are needed to make a profit mining crypto. However, as the speed of computers gets faster and faster, many users in the future may be able to mine from home with minimal investment. By having more users, mine with less investment. The technology will spread.

Crypto mining will also gain popularity due to the profit it generates for the user. Many people are looking for various ways to earn money or points they can use to purchase goods and services. If crypto mining can become something we can do on our smartphones or home computers, more users will try it to get these rewards. Similar to a points card, users will be able to crypto mine from day to day activities.

Crypto mining will become and remain popular because it can become a global currency. When traveling, we have to convert money to the local currency. This can cause us to lose money in the conversion. However, by having a digital currency, we can skip this process and use our money more freely around the world.

Crypto mining is still in its early days, however the future looks bright. Crypto mining will continue to expand and develop in popularity because technology is constantly advancing. It is also a great way for a person to earn extra income and use it across the world.

**Pro teams:** Brainstorm ideas that support your argument. Include data or research to strengthen your points.

– **Crypto mining benefits the environment...**
– **More cryptocurrencies will help it gain popularity...**

_____

_____

**Con teams:** Brainstorm ideas that support your argument. Include data or research to strengthen your points.

**– Crypto mining is damaging the environment…**
**– More cryptocurrencies will hurt its popularity…**

_____

_____

---

### Next, let's come up with our own arguments.

**Debate Theme 2:** Will crypto mining reach a limit where it is not cost effective?

**Debate Theme 3:** Are cryptocurrencies just a current fad similar to NFTs?

## 7. Mini-Research

Next, let's utilize the information we've learned so far on the topic and research some future questions about this news story. After doing some reseach, select the skills you want to practice with options A or B. Read the instructions carefully.

### A. Writing a short essay:

Work on your writing and create a short essay (Minimum of 500 words). This short essay should include information from your research and your ideas in your own words.

### B. Speaking and giving a slide presentation:

Work on your speaking and presentation skills by creating a 3 minute slide presentation. This slide presentation should include information from your research and your ideas in your own words.

**Review the following themes and select one to focus on:**

**Theme 1:** What is the future of crypto mining and cryptocurrencies?

**Theme 2:** Is digital currency dangerous to a country's economy?

**Theme 3:** Will more digital currencies spark more scams?

**Theme 4:** Do crypto mines hurt consumer electronic prices?

**Theme 5:** Do cryptocurrencies encourage or support illegal activities?

## 8. Project

**Using all the information we have learned so far in this lesson, let's combine what we have learned and organize a final project.**

**Review the following Project Prompts and select the one that interests you:**

**Project Prompt 1**   Explore the rising trend of using renewable energy sources for electricity generation. Research and propose novel and innovative methods for energy generation that may have previously seemed unnecessary.

**Project Prompt 2**   As technology continues to advance, the potential for electricity scarcity in the future is a concern. In this situation, what factors would you give priority to? Offer an explanation based on your reasoning.

After selecting your prompt, create your response in the form of a strong persuasive and engaging report. This report can include your thoughts in writing, data collection and analysis, as well as information from today's discussion.

# Population Decline

## 1. Check In

Let's start our lesson by describing your experience(s) relating to our topic for today's unit.

1. What are some challenges parents face raising children in today's society?
2. What are some ways the government can help encourage people to build larger families?

## 2. Listening Exercise 1: Opening paragraph

South Korea has the world's tenth largest economy, but it's facing a big problem. Where to find workers in a country with the lowest birthrate in the world. As Paula Hancocks reports the problem is rooted in cultural attitude about the rule of women. And the government isn't really helping.

### What's next in the story?

**From the listening exercise, answer the following questions.**

1. What do you think this news story will be about?
2. What are some keywords you think will be important to this story?

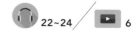

Watch the following news video and answer the questions in the next page.

SLUMPING BIRTHRATE

LIVE

SOUTH KOREA STRUGGLES WITH LOWEST FERTILITY RATE IN WORLD

CNN

7:20 AM GMT

1. **What is the purpose of the news story?**

    a.  To explain the complex issue of population decline in South Korea

    b.  To introduce new government programs to support single parents in South Korea

    c.  To explain why South Korean women are not seeking marriage or relationships

    d.  To talk about the challenges South Koreans face raising children


2. **The phrase "patriarchal society" is in the news story. Which option has the closest in meaning to:**

    a.  A society where women have equal rights and opportunities as men.

    b.  A society where women have more rights and opportunities than men.

    c.  A society where women hold more power and authority.

    d.  A society where men hold more power and authority.


3. **From the news story, what is the major concern regarding South Korea's aging population?**

    a.  The increasing costs of education as more schools close down.

    b.  The increase in women not wanting to get married and have children.

    c.  A lack of new workers putting money in the pension system.

    d.  Real estate costs rising resulting in many people not being able to afford housing.

## 4. Listening Exercise 3: Comprehension

Using the information you learned in the news story, select the best answer for each question.

1. According to the news report, the cost of education is an important factor in South Korea's low birth rate.

   a. True

   b. False

2. According to the news report, one solution to the problem is to provide more financial support to couples.

   a. True

   b. False

3. According to the news report, a South Korean joke compares a single woman to something nonhuman.

   a. True

   b. False

4. In the news report, what prevents men from helping out more?

   a. Men are often absent from their children's lives.

   b. Men work far from home and usually live away from their families.

   c. Men follow business culture where overwork is expected.

   d. Men are not knowledgeable with household chores.

5. According to Professor Cho Hae-Kyung, how are single mothers treated in South Korea?

   a. They are given additional support and special benefits.

   b. They are looked down on and viewed negatively.

   c. They are supported and seen as strong and independent.

   d. They are not treated in any special way.

6. According to the news story, what reason does Lee Jin-Song have for women avoiding marriage and children?

   a. Men and women are working more, which gives them fewer chances to interact, date, and socialize.

   b. Women over the age of 25 are seen as less desirable for men.

   c. The economy is making it more difficult for people, especially couples, to buy homes.

   d. Women view marriage as a lot of work which involves giving up a lot of their future.

## 5. Creating a Summary

Look at the options below and select A or B. Read the instructions carefully.

**A. Writing and creating an infographic:**

Work on your writing and organizational skills by creating a poster presentation. This poster should include the main ideas of the news article written in your own words. Organize your information and data points as an infographic.

**B. Speaking and giving a presentation:**

Work on your speaking and presenting skills by creating a 2 minute pitch talk. This will be a short speech which includes a summary of the main ideas of the news article written in your own words. How can you get others to understand this news story?

## 6. Debate Exercise

Let's discuss the topic further by having a debate. Split your class into groups and decide which group will be pro or con. The pro side will argue for the topic while the con side will argue against it.

Let's look at the following debate question

"Should countries do more to stop population decline?"

**Example Con Argument**

 25

### Should countries do more to stop population decline?

Countries should allow their citizens the freedom to do what they want to do. As society grows and evolves, we need to adjust to new attitudes towards traditional mindsets. Countries should not do more to combat population decline because we have a steady increase in the number of people around the world, support programs would be very costly, and it's very difficult to find the root cause of the problem from culture to culture.

Countries should have more of a global perspective. While it is true that some countries' populations are declining, there are other countries where it is increasing. This increasing global population has led to major problems in food disparity where some countries have too much while others have too little. It is important to look at the bigger picture.

Countries may want to try to solve population problems with social programs. There are many countries trying a variety of methods to support married couples financially by providing cheaper daycare costs or funding with education. However, these programs are very costly and not always effective. Some problems require more than just money.

Finding the core cause of population decline is difficult because we have to consider each country's culture. Some countries have a strong work culture where people are expected to stay beyond regular work hours while other countries have different work dynamics. Family culture also varies from country to country. There are many factors we have to consider and there is no one-size-fits-all solution to this issue. Due to this, countries face challenges trying to tackle this complex issue.

Countries should think globally and avoid trying to solve overly complicated issues. Although some countries may see a population decline, others will see a boom. Countries also vary wildly in their business and daily life culture. It is due to these difficult reasons that countries should not waste resources trying to solve this problem.

**Pro teams:** Brainstorm ideas that support your argument. Include data or research to strengthen your points.

– **Countries should do more to stop population decline...**
– **More support programs should be created for parents...**

**Con teams:** Brainstorm ideas that support your argument. Include data or research to strengthen your points.

– **Countries should not do more to stop population decline...**
– **There should not be additional support programs for parents...**

---

### Next, let's come up with our own arguments.

**Debate Theme 2:** Is population decline a cultural problem?
**Debate Theme 3:** Will the idea of traditional marriage change in the future?

## 7. Mini-Research

**Next, let's utilize the information we've learned so far on the topic and research some future questions about this news story. After doing some reseach, select the skills you want to practice with options A or B. Read the instructions carefully.**

### A. Writing a short essay:

Work on your writing and create a short essay (Minimum of 500 words). This short essay should include information from your research and your ideas in your own words.

### B. Speaking and giving a slide presentation:

Work on your speaking and presentation skills by creating a 3 minute slide presentation. This slide presentation should include information from your research and your ideas in your own words.

**Review the following themes and select one to focus on:**

**Theme 1:** Population decline is as serious a problem as global warming.

**Theme 2:** What countries suffer the most from population decline and why?

**Theme 3:** What countries have recovered from population decline? What did they do to solve the problem?

**Theme 4:** Does work culture need to change in order to promote healthier family lifestyles?

**Theme 5:** How much does the economy impact population decline?

## 8. Project

Using all the information we have learned so far in this lesson, let's combine what we have learned and organize a final project.

**Review the following Project Prompts and select the one that interests you:**

**Project Prompt 1**   What measures have countries that effectively raised their birth rates implemented? Do you think that adopting similar measures would result in an increase in the birth rate in Japan?

**Project Prompt 2**   Explore innovations that have the potential to significantly boost the birth rate.

After selecting your prompt, create your response in the form of a strong persuasive and engaging report. This report can include your thoughts in writing, data collection and analysis, as well as information from today's discussion.

Unit 6

# Global Warming

### 1. Check In

**Let's start our lesson by describing your experience(s) relating to our topic for today's unit.**

1.  Have you heard of climate change? If so, what are your thoughts on it?
2.  In your experience, have you felt summers getting hotter or winters getting colder?

### 2. Listening Exercise 1: Opening paragraph

**COREN:** A sobering new analysis by climate scientists at the United Nations presents a grim picture of the future if global emissions are not slashed very soon.

CNN meteorologist Pedram Javaheri has a preview.

> **What's next in the story?**

**From the listening exercise, answer the following questions.**

1.  What do you think this news story will be about?
2.  What are some keywords you think will be important to this story?

## 3. Listening Exercise 2: Let's listen to the full story.

Watch the following news video and answer the questions in the next page.

1. **What is the purpose of the news story?**

    a. To explain global warming and how it is affecting the world

    b. To discuss the rise in temperature and how to manage it

    c. To show the trend of global warming over time and offer a warning

    d. To explain some positive points of global warming such as finding new animal species

2. **The word "threshold" is used by Pedram Javaheri. Which option has the closest in meaning to:**

    a. The line we cannot cross before the climate gets worse

    b. The limit that one company can produce that harms that environment

    c. Holding or limiting the amount a company can produce in a year

    d. Research that has been collected from various academic fields

3. **From the news story, what does Pedram Javaheri think of the future?**

    a. Scientists will find the solution to global warming.

    b. Countries will not meet their target goals for emissions.

    c. Violent storms and damage will increase.

    d. People will adjust to the new weather styles.

Using the information you learned in the news story, select the best answer for each question.

1. According to the news report, the United Nations has set a goal of a 45 percent cut to emissions in the next eight years.

   a. True
   b. False

2. According to the news report, the last seven years we have continuously broken temperature records.

   a. True
   b. False

3. According to the news report, the consequences of temperature increase are minor and manageable.

   a. True
   b. False

4. In the news story, what temperature increase is the Earth still projected to experience by 2100?

   a. Less than 1 degree Celsius
   b. Approximately 1.5 degrees Celsius
   c. More than 3 degrees Celsius
   d. Around 2 degrees Celsius

5. According to the news report, what types of energy are being promoted to incentivize businesses but leading to higher emissions?

   a. Nuclear power
   b. Wind and solar energy
   c. Biofuels and other developing technologies
   d. Coal, gas, and oil

6. At the end of the news report, the phrase "sobering news" is used after Pedram's report. Which of these options is the closest in meaning?

   a. News related to alcohol and drinking.
   b. News that discusses current events.
   c. News that introduces new findings or discoveries.
   d. News that is heavy and important.

## 5. Creating a Summary

**Look at the options below and select A or B. Read the instructions carefully.**

**A. Writing and creating an infographic:**

Work on your writing and organizational skills by creating a poster presentation. This poster should include the main ideas of the news article written in your own words. Organize your information and data points as an infographic.

**B. Speaking and giving a presentation:**

Work on your speaking and presenting skills by creating a 2 minute pitch talk. This will be a short speech which includes a summary of the main ideas of the news article written in your own words. How can you get others to understand this news story?

## 6. Debate Exercise

**Let's discuss the topic further by having a debate. Split your class into groups and decide which group will be pro or con. The pro side will argue for the topic while the con side will argue against it.**

Let's look at the following debate question

**"Is climate change preventable?"**

**Example Pro Argument**

 29

### Is climate change preventable?

Climate change is preventable. It will not be easy and will require a unification of all countries to achieve. Climate change can occur if we as a planet, work together, set reasonable goals for each country, and provide support to developing nations.

Climate change requires a global mindset.  This means we need to think not as a person from a country but as a person on this planet.  Countries and peoples will need to work together, sharing information and offering advice both positive and negative in order to improve.

Climate change will also require us to set reasonable goals.  These goals need to suit each country differently.  Since some countries are more advanced than others, we need to customize goals to suit each nation.  Countries with advanced technologies can pursue more sustainable energy while developing nations need to be allowed a chance to grow.

Finally, we need to provide support to developing nations.  Since many countries are growing and trying to become more modern.  It is important to provide them support since they will mainly be using environmentally unfriendly means of energy.  This requires countries to share their skills and support those that are smaller or weaker than them.

Climate change is a scary thing.  We are seeing higher and higher temperatures but we still lack a global mindset.  We can alter climate change but only if we cooperate, set clear objectives, and help each other.

**Pro teams:** Brainstorm ideas that support your argument.  Include data or research to strengthen your points.

**– Climate change is preventable because…**
**– There are many actions we can take to prevent climate change such as…**

_____

_____

**Con teams:** Brainstorm ideas that support your argument.  Include data or research to strengthen your points.

**– Climate change is unpreventable because…**
**– There are no significant actions we can take to prevent climate change because…**

_____

_____

## Next, let's come up with our own arguments.

**Debate Theme 2:** Climate change can be prevented with new developing technologies.

**Debate Theme 3:** Humans will adjust to climate change.

## 7. Mini-Research

**Next, let's utilize the information we've learned so far on the topic and research some future questions about this news story. After doing some reseach, select the skills you want to practice with options A or B. Read the instructions carefully.**

### A. Writing a short essay:

Work on your writing and create a short essay (Minimum of 500 words). This short essay should include information from your research and your ideas in your own words.

### B. Speaking and giving a slide presentation:

Work on your speaking and presentation skills by creating a 3 minute slide presentation. This slide presentation should include information from your research and your ideas in your own words.

**Review the following themes and select one to focus on:**

**Theme 1:** What actions should countries take to help them with climate change?

**Theme 2:** Should developing countries stop advancing to slow down climate change?

**Theme 3:** Should new emphasis be placed on technology for potential solutions to climate change?

**Theme 4:** Is climate change something that just happens naturally in Earth's history?

**Theme 5:** Is climate change a big deal or is it something we just need to get used to?

## 8. Project

**Using all the information we have learned so far in this lesson, let's combine what we have learned and organize a final project.**

**Review the following Project Prompts and select the one that interests you:**

**Project Prompt 1**   With numerous global efforts to reduce emissions, how do you predict that $CO_2$ emissions and global temperatures will change in the next 100 years? Provide your predictions along with the reasoning behind them.

**Project Prompt 2**   What do you regard as crucial in significantly reducing $CO_2$ emissions? Share specific proposals and suggestions on how to achieve these objectives.

After selecting your prompt, create your response in the form of a strong persuasive and engaging report. This report can include your thoughts in writing, data collection and analysis, as well as information from today's discussion.

# Shark Tourism

## 1. Check In

Let's start our lesson by describing your experience(s) relating to our topic for today's unit.

1. Are there any animals that scare or frighten you? If so, why?
2. What do you know of animal conservation?

## 2. Listening Exercise 1: Opening paragraph

**PATRICK OPPMANN, CNN CORRESPONDENT (voice-over):** Usually, they are the last thing you want to see in the ocean, but sharks are the reason why we have come here to the waters off Eastern Cuba. We're hoping to see the predators up close and with no cage. Local guides say this is the only place in Cuba, perhaps, one of only a handful in the world, where divers can safely swim alongside bull sharks.

### What's next in the story?

**From the listening exercise, answer the following questions.**

1. What do you think this news story will be about?
2. What are some keywords you think will be important to this story?

## 3. Listening Exercise 2: Let's listen to the full story.

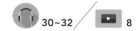 30~32 / 8

**Watch the following news video and answer the questions in the next page.**

Unit 8

1. **What is the purpose of the news story?**

    a. To discuss Cuba and the protection of sharks

    b. To introduce Cuba as a sightseeing spot for scuba diving

    c. To talk about the aggressive nature of the bull shark

    d. To show the growing popularity of shark diving

2. **The word "myth" is in the news story. Which option has the closest in meaning to:**

    a. A story which is based on facts and logic.

    b. A popular belief based on academic research.

    c. A fictional tale which provides a lesson.

    d. A widespread but false idea.

3. **From the news story, why did Cuba start putting in protections for sharks?**

    a. They wanted to start farming sharks for food.

    b. They saw them as a financial and environmental benefit.

    c. They wanted to research the bull sharks more deeply.

    d. They wanted to dispel people's fears of sharks from movies such as "Jaws".

Using the information you learned in the news story, select the best answer for each question.

1.  According to the news report, bull sharks are considered friendly and not aggressive.

    a.  True
    b.  False

2.  According to the news report, bull sharks provide great environmental benefits.

    a.  True
    b.  False

3.  According to the news report, Cuba is a rare place where divers can swim naturally with bull sharks.

    a.  True
    b.  False

4.  In the news report, what is the economic benefit for Cuba?

    a.  Cuban culture can become more mainstream.
    b.  Universities increase the amount of students who want to study sharks.
    c.  People pay to view the sharks and overcome their fears.
    d.  More research can be done to study sharks in their natural environment.

5.  In the news story, the phrase "considered a nuisance" is used by Patrick Oppmann. Which of these options is the closest in meaning?

    a.  To see something as positive
    b.  To have plenty of something
    c.  To be bothered by something
    d.  To feel scared of something

6.  How do the tourist guides attract bull sharks during the dives?

    a.  Guides provide large amounts of food to attract the sharks.
    b.  Guides create noise which attracts the curious sharks.
    c.  Guides hunt fish and provide small amounts to the sharks.
    d.  Guides feed the sharks medicine to keep them calm.

## 5. Creating a Summary

Look at the options below and select A or B. Read the instructions carefully.

**A. Writing and creating an infographic:**

Work on your writing and organizational skills by creating a poster presentation. This poster should include the main ideas of the news article written in your own words. Organize your information and data points as an infographic.

**B. Speaking and giving a presentation:**

Work on your speaking and presenting skills by creating a 2 minute pitch talk. This will be a short speech which includes a summary of the main ideas of the news article written in your own words. How can you get others to understand this news story?

## 6. Debate Exercise

Let's discuss the topic further by having a debate. Split your class into groups and decide which group will be pro or con. The pro side will argue for the topic while the con side will argue against it.

Let's look at the following debate question

**"Should more countries promote animal tourism?"**

**Example Pro Argument**

 33

### Should more countries promote animal tourism?

Animal tourism is a great way to expose and educate people to new creatures. Education is important for people to respect nature and understand our place in the world. Animal tourism should increase in countries to educate the public on rare species, break down negative images some animals have, and provide countries with economic benefits in the form of tourism.

Animal tourism can be a great educational tool. Many of us have fears of animals we do not normally get to see or interact with. Learning more about them can help us understand their behavior and overcome our fears. It is also a great way to build respect towards these creatures which will promote more animal protection.

Animal tourism can change our perspectives. As said earlier, many people have irrational fears of certain creatures. Certain creatures are associated with some stereotypes. For example, people may view spiders as dangerous when they can be extremely beneficial to the environment. Spiders eat smaller insects such as mosquitos which pose a much greater threat to human beings.

Animal tourism can provide a great source of income for certain countries. As COVID has died down, tourism will be increasing. This means more tourists will be traveling looking for activities and things to do. Using your local environment and showing animals can be a great way to build up the economy of exotic locations with rare species. This fresh income can be used to help protect local countries' resources as well as improve the lives of many animals.

In conclusion, animal tourism should be expanded to different areas. It is a great way to generate income as well as educate people and eliminate fears. With more animal species being in danger of global climate change this can be a great first step to providing them with much needed protection.

**Pro teams:** Brainstorm ideas that support your argument. Include data or research to strengthen your points.

– **Animal tourism should be expanded...**
– **Shark diving without cages should increase...**

**Con teams:** Brainstorm ideas that support your argument. Include data or research to strengthen your points.

– **Animal tourism should not be expanded...**
– **Shark diving without cages should decrease...**

_____

_____

> ## Next, let's come up with our own arguments.

**Debate Theme 2:** Should animals be used for tourism or left alone?

**Debate Theme 3:** Are animals our responsibility to protect?

## 7. Mini-Research

**Next, let's utilize the information we've learned so far on the topic and research some future questions about this news story. After doing some reseach, select the skills you want to practice with options A or B. Read the instructions carefully.**

**A. Writing a short essay:**

Work on your writing and create a short essay (Minimum of 500 words). This short essay should include information from your research and your ideas in your own words.

**B. Speaking and giving a slide presentation:**

Work on your speaking and presentation skills by creating a 3 minute slide presentation. This slide presentation should include information from your research and your ideas in your own words.

**Review the following themes and select one to focus on:**

**Theme 1:** What actions should countries take to protect animals and the environment?

**Theme 2:** Is animal tourism morally good or is it using animals as a product?

**Theme 3:** How much protection should countries provide certain species of animal?

**Theme 4:** What animals are the most feared and why? Is it justified?

**Theme 5:** Should people just leave nature alone or become more involved in its care?

## 8. Project

**Using all the information we have learned so far in this lesson, let's combine what we have learned and organize a final project.**

**Review the following Project Prompts and select the one that interests you:**

**Project Prompt 1**   Direct our attention to elements that have been overlooked in the past and propose innovative ideas for tourism that will attract people.

**Project Prompt 2**   While there is a growing number of exciting plans to attract tourists, concerns related to tourism are also increasing in many locations. Let's examine these challenges and discuss potential solutions for sustainable tourism.

After selecting your prompt, create your response in the form of a strong persuasive and engaging report. This report can include your thoughts in writing, data collection and analysis, as well as information from today's discussion.

# Scams and Robocalling

CNNI 40001
Inews Printer 124

## 1. Check In

Let's start our lesson by describing your experience(s) relating to our topic for today's unit.

1.  Have you ever received unwanted phone calls or spam messages? If so, what did you do?

2.  What precautions or protections do you think we need when using online technologies?

## 2. Listening Exercise 1: Opening paragraph

BRUNHUBER: Well, the phone calls have become so common they've turned into a sort of running joke in the United States. But they are no laughing matter for many people who have lost money to the millions of scam robocalls made last year in the U.S. And as our Gabe Cohen reports, it's an uphill battle to shut them down.

### What's next in the story?

From the listening exercise, answer the following questions.

1.  What do you think this news story will be about?

2.  What are some keywords you think will be important to this story?

## 3. Listening Exercise 2: Let's listen to the full story.

Watch the following news video and answer the questions in the next page.

1. **What is the purpose of the news story?**

    a. To explain robocalling and its everyday applications in our lives

    b. To discuss a lawsuit against two men who ran a robocalling operation

    c. To show how these robocalling scams work to trick people and get their money

    d. To introduce new technology which will protect against robocalling

2. **The phrase "slap on the wrist" is used by Dave Yost.  Which option has the closest in meaning to:**

    a. Causing serious physical harm on someone

    b. Causing light physical harm on someone

    c. A light penalty for a crime

    d. A heavy penalty for a crime

3. **From the news story, how will the future of robocalling be handled?**

    a. They are going to put stronger laws into place with harsher penalties for criminals.

    b. Putting more effort into tracking down the scammers overseas with foreign government officials.

    c. Focusing on the telephone companies which can track and block these unwanted calls.

    d. To develop more technology to identify where calls are coming from and who to target.

**Listening Exercise 3:** Comprehension

Using the information you learned in the news story, select the best answer for each question.

1.  According to the news report, the two men robocalling operation affected exactly 8 million people.

    a.  True
    b.  False

2.  According to the news report, robocalling cost Americans almost 40 billion dollars in one year.

    a.  True
    b.  False

3.  According to the news report, after working with telecom industries, robocalling and scams almost disappeared.

    a.  True
    b.  False

4.  What explanation does the article give for robocall scammers to continue even after being caught?

    a.  Scammers have no other opportunities to make money so they continue with new scripts.
    b.  The punishment for getting caught is a small fine so it doesn't bother scammers.
    c.  Many scammers are never truly caught so they continue with new names and identities.
    d.  Many scammers have equipment which is specialized and easy to apply to new scams.

5.  How has the American government responded to the issue of robocalls and scamming?

    a.  They have created a new group which will focus on tracking down these robocalls.
    b.  They are developing AI software which will mimic human language to deter scammers.
    c.  They are tracking down robocalling related hardware to find scamming centers.
    d.  They are working together with countries from overseas to try and come up with a solution.

6.  In the news story, Jessica Rosenworcel believes companies are "turning a blind eye" to this situation. What does she mean by this phrase?

    a.  Companies are not able to find or track these robocalling centers or scammers.
    b.  Companies don't have the tools to track down the information needed to stop this problem.
    c.  Companies are ignoring the problem instead of trying to work with others to solve it.
    d.  Companies are closing down support for these situations because they are too difficult.

Unit 9

## 5. Creating a Summary

Look at the options below and select A or B. Read the instructions carefully.

**A. Writing and creating an infographic:**

Work on your writing and organizational skills by creating a poster presentation. This poster should include the main ideas of the news article written in your own words. Organize your information and data points as an infographic.

**B. Speaking and giving a presentation:**

Work on your speaking and presenting skills by creating a 2 minute pitch talk. This will be a short speech which includes a summary of the main ideas of the news article written in your own words. How can you get others to understand this news story?

## 6. Debate Exercise

Let's discuss the topic further by having a debate. Split your class into groups and decide which group will be pro or con. The pro side will argue for the topic while the con side will argue against it.

> Let's look at the following debate question

"What will the future of robocalling and scams be? Will the government be able to stop this problem?"

**Example Con Argument**

37

### What will the future of robocalling and scams be? Will the government be able to stop this problem?

Robocalling and scams will always exist. We can try to stop these but people will always have a chance of being tricked. Scamming will always exist and there is nothing we can do to stop it because it is flexible, difficult to catch, and makes people a lot of money.

Robocalling and scamming require scripts which trick the listener into paying money. These tricks can come in many different forms. In the news story, they mentioned a car loan but this can also be easily changed to a bill such as an electric bill or water bill. With this flexibility, it is very hard to stop.

Scamming is also very difficult to catch. With phones and online communications becoming more common it is easy for people from different countries to communicate. This communication can lead to scamming across the world. This will require a global unit which will be very difficult to maintain.

Finally, scamming makes people money. As the news story mentioned, over 40 billion dollars was received in only one year. This is also one country, America, being the victim. This means a lot of countries are benefiting from more income and wealth. This makes it difficult to control.

In summary, robocalling and scamming will always exist in some form. It is too profitable, difficult to track, and the users can be from anywhere. Instead of policing this idea, we should encourage education especially among people who are the most likely to fall for these traps.

**Pro teams:** Brainstorm ideas that support your argument. Include data or research to strengthen your points.

– **Catching these criminals will improve with technology...**
– **Education on these scams can help stop them in the future...**

**Con teams:** Brainstorm ideas that support your argument. Include data or research to strengthen your points.

– **Criminals will use new technology to improve their scams...**
– **Education on these scams will help scammers adjust and find new weak points...**

## Next, let's come up with our own arguments.

**Debate Theme 2:** Robocalling and scams will decrease in the future.

**Debate Theme 3:** Robocalling and scams will increase in the future.

## 7. Mini-Research

**Next, let's utilize the information we've learned so far on the topic and research some future questions about this news story. After doing some reseach, select the skills you want to practice with options A or B. Read the instructions carefully.**

**A. Writing a short essay:**

Work on your writing and create a short essay (Minimum of 500 words). This short essay should include information from your research and your ideas in your own words.

**B. Speaking and giving a slide presentation:**

Work on your speaking and presentation skills by creating a 3 minute slide presentation. This slide presentation should include information from your research and your ideas in your own words.

**Review the following themes and select one to focus on:**

**Theme 1:** What are some robocalls or scams you are familiar with? What are the most common?

**Theme 2:** What are some effective ways to educate people to avoid scams?

**Theme 3:** As digital information grows, will more people be impacted by scams in the future?

**Theme 4:** Aside from the government, what other measures can we take to ensure the safety of people and their money?

**Theme 5:** With phones and phone calling on the decline, what do you imagine future scams will look like?

## 8. Project

**Using all the information we have learned so far in this lesson, let's combine what we have learned and organize a final project.**

**Review the following Project Prompts and select the one that interests you:**

**Project Prompt 1**   What do you believe are effective uses for technology-based phone systems? Consider practical applications and offer suggestions.

**Project Prompt 2**   The service that allows outgoing calls with different numbers is convenient, but it's also vulnerable to misuse in robocall scams. Similarly, what other systems do you think are convenient but could be at risk of misuse in the future?

After selecting your prompt, create your response in the form of a strong persuasive and engaging report. This report can include your thoughts in writing, data collection and analysis, as well as information from today's discussion.

**Unit 10**

# Food Inflation

## 1. Check In

Let's start our lesson by describing your experience(s) relating to our topic for today's unit.

1. Have you noticed any increases in the foods you purchase? If so, what?
2. What is the minimum wage for a part-time job?  What jobs interest you?

## 2. Listening Exercise 1: Opening paragraph

**COREN:** Rising food and energy prices in the U.K. who have been the largest contributor to inflation hitting a record high in the region. And Goldman Sachs warns that number could climb higher next year.

CNN's Scott McLean spoke with pensioners in London trying to stretch their government checks as far as possible amid the rising prices.

> What's next in the story?

**From the listening exercise, answer the following questions.**

1. What do you think this news story will be about?
2. What are some keywords you think will be important to this story?

Watch the following news video and answer the questions in the next page.

1. **What is the purpose of the news story?**

   a. To discuss how the world is dealing with inflation from families to the elderly

   b. To show how costs of items such as food can have a big impact

   c. To introduce how the elderly are handling their free time by playing games

   d. To show the benefits of a free bus pass as a form of keeping busy

2. **The word "inflation" is in the news story. Which option has the closest in meaning to:**

   a. Economic growth and increase of goods

   b. Economic decline and decrease of goods

   c. Lowered costs for foods and services

   d. Increased costs for foods and services

3. **From the news story, why are people, especially the elderly, spending their time riding the bus?**

   a. Buses provide a comfortable place to stay and enjoy the day without cost.

   b. There are many sightseeing spots which can be viewed from the bus route.

   c. The bus is a comfortable place to sleep to get to your destination.

   d. Buses are popular in the United Kingdom and many take photos of them.

## 4. Listening Exercise 3: Comprehension

Using the information you learned in the news story, select the best answer for each question.

1. According to the news report, the hot topic for the seniors in London is travel.

   a. True

   b. False

2. According to the news report, food inflation in the United Kingdom is 10 percent.

   a. True

   b. False

3. According to the news report, costs have made people decide to heat only the rooms they are using.

   a. True

   b. False

4. In the news report, how does Kenneth Bedford benefit from meals at the senior center?

   a. They are healthier since they are made from a professional chef.

   b. Kenneth cannot cook so he relies on the senior center for meals.

   c. The senior center offers a large variety of dishes.

   d. The cost is less than it would be if Kenneth cooked at home.

5. In the news story, the phrase "walks a tightrope" is used by Scott McLean. Which of these options is the closest in meaning?

   a. To be in a dangerous situation

   b. To balance things carefully

   c. To be entertaining to others

   d. To move casually through a situation

6. What decision will the Prime Minister Rishi Sunak have to make?

   a. Raise state pensions in line with inflation

   b. Provide additional subsidies for food prices

   c. Decrease taxes on energy expenses

   d. Raise overall income for part-time and full-time employees

## 5. Creating a Summary

Look at the options below and select A or B. Read the instructions carefully.

**A. Writing and creating an infographic:**

Work on your writing and organizational skills by creating a poster presentation. This poster should include the main ideas of the news article written in your own words. Organize your information and data points as an infographic.

**B. Speaking and giving a presentation:**

Work on your speaking and presenting skills by creating a 2 minute pitch talk. This will be a short speech which includes a summary of the main ideas of the news article written in your own words. How can you get others to understand this news story?

## 6. Debate Exercise

Let's discuss the topic further by having a debate. Split your class into groups and decide which group will be pro or con. The pro side will argue for the topic while the con side will argue against it.

Let's look at the following debate question

"Can countries handle and manage the impact of inflation?"

**Example Pro Argument**

41

### Can countries handle and manage the impact of inflation?

Inflation is a growing problem around the world. Many countries are currently suffering from inflation. However, inflation has happened in the past and will continue to happen into the future. Countries can only handle inflation by supporting their citizens with support programs, providing reasonable economic guidance, and offering moral support.

Inflation needs to be countered with strong support programs for those most affected. This includes groups like the elderly or people who are struggling with poverty. Inflation affects these groups the most because they have limited resources and are not able to work and have an income. These programs can come in many forms such as food programs, housing and shelter, as well as donations for daily use goods.

Countries should also provide strong economic guidance. This means they should let their people know the details of the situation and explain the best strategies to handle these difficult times. Many people lack economic awareness so it is important to keep the citizens educated so they can budget accordingly.

Finally, countries need to provide strong moral support during these tough times. Inflation imposes a lot of stress on the population, and with no strong outlook to the future, it is difficult to help people keep a positive mindset. Moral support can come in many forms but strong leadership and a plan into the future will help people keep moving forward.

Inflation is a difficult topic. However, we can look at history to see how people have handled these situations in the past. Strong support programs, education, and moral support can help people get through these tough times.

**Pro teams:** Brainstorm ideas that support your argument. Include data or research to strengthen your points.

– **Countries can manage inflation because...**
– **Inflation is a natural global phenomenon...**

**Con teams:** Brainstorm ideas that support your argument. Include data or research to strengthen your points.

– **Countries cannot handle inflation because...**
– **Inflation is not a natural global phenomenon...**

## Next, let's come up with our own arguments.

**Debate Theme 2:** Is inflation a permanent problem or a temporary one?

**Debate Theme 3:** Are inflation and economic inequality linked?

## 7. Mini-Research

**Next, let's utilize the information we've learned so far on the topic and research some future questions about this news story. After doing some reseach, select the skills you want to practice with options A or B. Read the instructions carefully.**

### A.  Writing a short essay:

Work on your writing and create a short essay (Minimum of 500 words). This short essay should include information from your research and your ideas in your own words.

### B.  Speaking and giving a slide presentation:

Work on your speaking and presentation skills by creating a 3 minute slide presentation. This slide presentation should include information from your research and your ideas in your own words.

**Review the following themes and select one to focus on:**

**Theme 1:**   What actions should countries take to handle inflation?

**Theme 2:**   Is inflation or rising prices more of a problem than deflation or the falling of prices?

**Theme 3:**   How have countries handled inflation in the past?

**Theme 4:**   What is the best advice you would give to someone struggling with rising prices?

**Theme 5:**   Is inflation necessary for economic growth?  As societies get richer, so does the cost of their goods and services.

# 8. Project

Using all the information we have learned so far in this lesson, let's combine what we have learned and organize a final project.

**Review the following Project Prompts and select the one that interests you:**

**Project Prompt 1**    Propose an alternative pension plan that could replace the Japanese Pension System.

**Project Prompt 2**    Consider creating a retirement savings plan that accounts for your future financial needs. Determine the specific amount of money you will require and evaluate your savings strategy accordingly.

After selecting your prompt, create your response in the form of a strong persuasive and engaging report. This report can include your thoughts in writing, data collection and analysis, as well as information from today's discussion.

# Driving Safe

## 1. Check In

**Let's start our lesson by describing your experience(s) relating to our topic for today's unit.**

1. Have you ever felt in danger from cars on the road?
2. How do you stay safe from vehicles when driving your bicycle or walking on the street?

## 2. Listening Exercise 1: Opening paragraph

**Announcer:** Ok, well, thousands of road deaths each year from unsafe driving has prompted some companies to develop new technology that could help keep you safe but actually control the speed of the vehicle. Some users say the privacy of drivers is now at risk.

CNN's Pete Muntean has more.

### What's next in the story?

**From the listening exercise, answer the following questions.**

1. What do you think this news story will be about?
2. What are some keywords you think will be important to this story?

**3.** **Listening Exercise 2:** Let's listen to the full story.  42~44 / ▶ 11

**Watch the following news video and answer the questions in the next page.**

NEW TECHNOLOGY
DEVICE ON CARS STOPS DRIVERS FROM EXCEEDING SPEED LIMIT
LIVE
CNN
KOSPI ▼ -46.78

Unit 11

1. **What is the purpose of the news story?**

    a.  To introduce electric cars and their gaining popularity as well as their new features

    b.  To explain a new New York law for all cars requiring vehicles to slow down

    c   To describe how this new car technology works to slow vehicles down

    d.  To introduce anti speeding technology and discuss the ethics of it

2. **The word "incentivizing" is used by Pete Muntean. Which option has the closest in meaning to:**

    a.  Motivating

    b.  Inventing

    c.  Adding on

    d.  Penalizing

3. **From the news story, how do people feel about this new car technology?**

    a.  People are extremely supportive of the idea and technology.

    b.  People are extremely against the idea and technology.

    c.  Opinions differ from person to person on the idea and technology.

    d.  People feel indifferent because the technology is already used in Europe.

Using the information you learned in the news story, select the best answer for each question.

1.  According to the news report, the Intelligent Speed Assistance technology will limit the car to 20 miles per hour (mph).

    a.  True
    b.  False

2.  According to the news report, there have been more than 20,000 deaths in only 6 months due to road incidences.

    a.  True
    b.  False

3.  According to the news report, New York city will be a testing ground for this new type of technology.

    a.  True
    b.  False

4.  In the news story, the phrase "a lead foot" is used by Pete Muntean.  Which of these options is the closest in meaning?

    a.  A person's dominant hand or foot (such as left or right handed).
    b.  Using your foot to guide the way to a destination.
    c.  Using your foot too heavily or strongly while driving.
    d.  The part of the car designed to make your foot more comfortable.

5.  How does the telematics speed program technology work?

    a.  It checks how fast the car is moving and will cause a dead pedal if the car goes beyond 20 mph.
    b.  Using multiple cars, everyone's speed can be collected and then averaged out to make sure everyone is going at a similar pace.
    c.  It uses a black button to the left of the driver and cuts off the accelerator to avoid you from going too fast.
    d.  It checks the car's location as well as the local regional legal speed and then will adjust your speed settings.

6. In the news story, what does the industry expert Karl Brauer think about this new technology?

   a. People are going to love the new features but it will take them time to learn how to use it.

   b. People will feel this too extreme at first but this will eventually be the new normal.

   c. Companies will not want to participate due to costs and putting a stop to their sales.

   d. Karl thinks this technology is still far in the future and does not think we will see it soon.

## 5. Creating a Summary

**Look at the options below and select A or B. Read the instructions carefully.**

### A. Writing and creating an infographic:

Work on your writing and organizational skills by creating a poster presentation. This poster should include the main ideas of the news article written in your own words. Organize your information and data points as an infographic.

### B. Speaking and giving a presentation:

Work on your speaking and presenting skills by creating a 2 minute pitch talk. This will be a short speech which includes a summary of the main ideas of the news article written in your own words. How can you get others to understand this news story?

## 6. Debate Exercise

**Let's discuss the topic further by having a debate. Split your class into groups and decide which group will be pro or con. The pro side will argue for the topic while the con side will argue against it.**

> Let's look at the following debate question

**"Should all cars have this technology installed in their cars?"**

**Example Pro Argument**

## Should all cars have this technology installed in their cars?

As cars and technology become more advanced, it is important for us to utilize all tools available to make the road as safe as possible. This is why we should install this new speed technology in every vehicle on the road. It will cause less speeding, less accidents, and people will get more familiar with new technology.

Using this technology will reduce speeding. Since the car calculates where you are and how fast you should be going, it will provide many people with more awareness on how they drive. Some people drive fast by nature, so this will be a great opportunity for them to learn about their bad habits. This will also lead to safer driving.

This technology will also reduce accidents on the road. Many accidents on streets/roads are caused by speed and carelessness. By limiting how fast we can go, more people will be aware of what they are doing. They will also be more cautious with their driving.

Finally, this new technology is just one of many new technologies which are being developed and implemented in our daily lives. All new technology meets resistance at first as people are uncomfortable with sudden changes to their daily life. It will take time but this new technology will be a great way to make cars and other vehicles safer.

In conclusion, speed reducing technology will be a great tool for everyone. It will make people aware of the speeds that they drive, reduce the number of people injured, and will be a great starting point to introduce other features for safer driving. No one should fear the road.

**Pro teams:** Brainstorm ideas that support your argument. Include data or research to strengthen your points.

**– This technology will reduce accidents...**
**– This technology will become widespread because...**

**Con teams:** Brainstorm ideas that support your argument. Include data or research to strengthen your points.

– **This technology will increase accidents...**

– **This technology will not become widespread because...**

_____

_____

### Next, let's come up with our own arguments.

**Debate Theme 2:** This technology and others such as self driving cars will increase in the future.

**Debate Theme 3:** Humans should always have control of their vehicles.

## 7. Mini-Research

**Next, let's utilize the information we've learned so far on the topic and research some future questions about this news story. After doing some reseach, select the skills you want to practice with options A or B. Read the instructions carefully.**

**A. Writing a short essay:**

Work on your writing and create a short essay (Minimum of 500 words). This short essay should include information from your research and your ideas in your own words.

**B. Speaking and giving a slide presentation:**

Work on your speaking and presentation skills by creating a 3 minute slide presentation. This slide presentation should include information from your research and your ideas in your own words.

**Review the following themes and select one to focus on:**

**Theme 1:** What are some other safety features you feel should be implemented?

**Theme 2:** Should age requirements be set for driving on the road?

**Theme 3:** As technology advances, are self driving cars inevitable?

**Theme 4:** What would you consider "overreach" by the government?

**Theme 5:** Were all safety features welcomed by people at their start? (seat belts, airbags, etc.)

## 8. Project

**Using all the information we have learned so far in this lesson, let's combine what we have learned and organize a final project.**

**Review the following Project Prompts and select the one that interests you:**

**Project Prompt 1**   Imagine the future of urban transportation. What does the transportation landscape look like in 2050?

**Project Prompt 2**   Offer a visionary plan to nurture a society where legal regulations and moral principles coexist in harmony, fostering a more compassionate community.

> After selecting your prompt, create your response in the form of a strong persuasive and engaging report. This report can include your thoughts in writing, data collection and analysis, as well as information from today's discussion.

# COVID-19 Lockdowns

## 1. Check In

**Let's start our lesson by describing your experience(s) relating to our topic for today's unit.**

1. How did COVID affect your day to day life?
2. What precautions did you need to take during the peak of COVID? Online classes, masks, etc?

## 2. Listening Exercise 1: Opening paragraph

**BRUNHUBER:** The latest video from social media shows residents in cities across China tearing down those big metal barricades used by police to enforce COVID lockdowns.

CNN's Selina Wang spoke with one protester and asked him what he hopes to accomplish. Listen to this.

| What's next in the story? |
| --- |

**From the listening exercise, answer the following questions.**

1. What do you think this news story will be about?
2. What are some keywords you think will be important to this story?

## 3. Listening Exercise 2: Let's listen to the full story.

🎧 46~48 ▶️ 12

**Watch the following news video and answer the questions in the next page.**

Unit 12

1. **What is the purpose of the news story?**

    a.  To inform the audience about the recent rise in COVID cases in China.

    b.  To highlight the political unrest and protests in China due to COVID lockdowns.

    c.  To discuss the economic impact of the COVID lockdowns on Chinese residents.

    d.  To show the effectiveness of China's zero-COVID policy in controlling the pandemic.

2. **The word "censor" is in the news story to describe China's reaction to protests. Which option has the closest in meaning to:**

    a.  To limit or block information in the media

    b.  To spread and share information in the media

    c.  To block or barricade areas of the city

    d.  To protest and carry a white piece of paper

3. **From the news story, what does the white paper many Chinese protesters hold represent?**

    a.  An appeal to the international community to help with China's strict COVID policies.

    b.  A demand for increased healthcare resources to combat the pandemic.

    c.  A sign of surrender to the Chinese government to avoid more violence.

    d.  A simple symbol that represents deleted material and government censorship.

## 4. Listening Exercise 3: Comprehension

Using the information you learned in the news story, select the best answer for each question.

1. According to the news report, The protester interviewed asked for the resignation of China's president, Xi Jinping.

   a. True

   b. False

2. According to the news report, Chinese authorities openly supported the demonstrators' right to express their grievances.

   a. True

   b. False

3. According to the news report, citizens of Shanghai were stopped and had their phones checked by police in search of banned communication apps.

   a. True

   b. False

4. In the news report, what happened in Guangzhou after residents destroyed COVID testing booths?

   a. The local residents were fined for their actions.

   b. The government lifted all lockdowns in the city.

   c. The protesters held talks with the authorities.

   d. The police gathered and got rid of the protestors.

5. According to the news report, why did the anonymous speaker fear these protests couldn't continue?

   a. VPNs were getting costly for citizens to continue using.

   b. Police were checking phones and also secretly joining protesting groups.

   c. Stronger barricades were being put into place to stop people from gathering.

   d. The punishment for protesting was getting more and more severe.

6. According to the news story, what did the protesters hope to achieve?

   a. They wanted to create a new and less oppressive system of government.

   b. They wanted to attract media attention and spread their message around the world.

   c. They wanted to improve the economic conditions of these locked down areas.

   d. They wanted the government to reconsider its COVID policies.

## 5. Creating a Summary

**Look at the options below and select A or B. Read the instructions carefully.**

**A. Writing and creating an infographic:**

Work on your writing and organizational skills by creating a poster presentation. This poster should include the main ideas of the news article written in your own words. Organize your information and data points as an infographic.

**B. Speaking and giving a presentation:**

Work on your speaking and presenting skills by creating a 2 minute pitch talk. This will be a short speech which includes a summary of the main ideas of the news article written in your own words. How can you get others to understand this news story?

## 6. Debate Exercise

**Let's discuss the topic further by having a debate. Split your class into groups and decide which group will be pro or con. The pro side will argue for the topic while the con side will argue against it.**

Let's look at the following debate question

**"Should governments have the power to enforce COVID lockdowns?"**

**Example Pro Argument**

 49

### Should governments have the power to enforce COVID lockdowns?

COVID lockdowns, while not popular, were extremely important in keeping people safe and the coronavirus from spreading. Though it may impact our daily life as well as local businesses, public health is more important. Governments should have the power to enforce COVID lockdowns because they reduce the spread of the coronavirus, allow time for governments to access the situation, and people can enjoy their freedoms once it ends.

COVID lockdowns reduce the spread of the coronavirus. By forcing people to stay indoors and in their living areas, the coronavirus cannot spread as easily as it could in regular living conditions. While challenging for the people involved, it is a necessary sacrifice to ensure public safety.

COVID lockdowns also allow more time for governments to manage the situation. COVID outbreaks can be wild and unpredictable. Isolating an area and preparing a plan is the best strategy to deal with such a dangerous virus. Emergency medical centers can be created nearby to provide quicker assistance to those suffering.

Finally, lockdowns are temporary measures. They are not meant to be permanent and after the lockdown is officially lifted, citizens can live their lives in peace knowing they are safe from the coronavirus. They can get back to all the activities they enjoy without worrying about getting sick.

COVID lockdowns are a complicated issue. They impact people's freedoms but they are necessary to ensure public health and safety. Sometimes we are not allowed to do the things we may want to for the greater good. Lockdowns help decrease the total number of COVID patients, provide time for governments to set up health measures, and when it is over people can go on with their lives.

**Pro teams:** Brainstorm ideas that support your argument. Include data or research to strengthen your points.

– **COVID lockdowns are beneficial...**
– **Masks should be required...**

_____

_____

**Con teams:** Brainstorm ideas that support your argument. Include data or research to strengthen your points.

– **COVID lockdowns are detrimental...**
– **Masks should not be required...**

_____

_____

## Next, let's come up with our own arguments.

**Debate Theme 2:** Do governments have the right to limit personal freedoms for the greater good of the public?

**Debate Theme 3:** Is protesting and civil disobedience okay in order to express negative feelings towards the government?

## 7. Mini-Research

**Next, let's utilize the information we've learned so far on the topic and research some future questions about this news story. After doing some reseach, select the skills you want to practice with options A or B. Read the instructions carefully.**

### A. Writing a short essay:

Work on your writing and create a short essay (Minimum of 500 words). This short essay should include information from your research and your ideas in your own words.

### B. Speaking and giving a slide presentation:

Work on your speaking and presentation skills by creating a 3 minute slide presentation. This slide presentation should include information from your research and your ideas in your own words.

**Review the following themes and select one to focus on:**

**Theme 1:** Is government censorship a growing problem? Are social platforms a public or private space?

**Theme 2:** Were countries who enforced strong COVID protocols better off than countries that did nothing?

**Theme 3:** Should countries who enforce strict lockdowns be responsible to support local businesses?

**Theme 4:** During a pandemic, should we be denied our personal freedoms to ensure public safety?

**Theme 5:** Should the government ever be allowed to force wearing a mask in public or any other "dangerous" activities?

## 8. Project

**Using all the information we have learned so far in this lesson, let's combine what we have learned and organize a final project.**

**Review the following Project Prompts and select the one that interests you:**

**Project Prompt 1**   When dealing with the future spread of infectious diseases like COVID-19, it is important to consider the implementation of suitable policies. To achieve this, analyze countermeasures adopted by other countries and take into account past policies to identify specific measures that the Japanese government should consider adopting.

**Project Prompt 2**   In addition to protests, what other methods do you believe can bring about societal change?

> After selecting your prompt, create your response in the form of a strong persuasive and engaging report. This report can include your thoughts in writing, data collection and analysis, as well as information from today's discussion.

## Unit 13

# LGBT Rights

## 1. Check In

**Let's start our lesson by describing your experience(s) relating to our topic for today's unit.**

1. What do you know about the LGBTQ movement?
2. How much should the government say in our relationship with others?

## 2. Listening Exercise 1: Opening paragraph

Russia is one step away from formally expanding its ban on what the government calls LGBT propaganda. The upper House of parliament passed a controversial bill Wednesday. Now it just needs President Vladimir Putin's signature as Fred Pleitgen reports the Kremlin is framing the move as part of a larger battle with the West.

### What's next in the story?

**From the listening exercise, answer the following questions.**

1. What do you think this news story will be about?
2. What are some keywords you think will be important to this story?

## 3. Listening Exercise 2: Let's listen to the full story.

50~52 / 13

**Watch the following news video and answer the questions in the next page.**

Unit 13

1. **What is the purpose of the news story?**

   a. To explain the potential impact of LGBTQ ideals on the Russian economy

   b. To describe how these new LGBTQ laws will impact foreign relations

   c. To identify the growing tensions between the West and Russia

   d. To discuss the dangers the LGBTQ community faces if they remain in Russia

2. **The word "scapegoat" is in the news story by Yaroslav Rasputin. Which option has the closest in meaning to:**

   a. A person who works with livestock.

   b. A person who is viewed as fearsome.

   c. A person where blame is shifted towards.

   d. A person who is guilty of a crime.

3. **From the news story, what is the major concern by activities and lawyers?**

   a. They are worried about the impact this will have on tourism.

   b. They are concerned individuals will need to flee to the country.

   c. They are worried about the economic impact on the country.

   d. They are worried LTBTQ ideologies will spread.

## 4. Listening Exercise 3: Comprehension

Using the information you learned in the news story, select the best answer for each question.

1.  According to the news report, Russian parliament has already passed the anti-LGBT propaganda bill.

    a.  True
    b.  False

2.  According to the news report, Russian President Vladimir Putin supports and promotes LGBTQ freedoms in Russia.

    a.  True
    b.  False

3.  According to the news report, there were some Russian legislators who voted against the controversial bill.

    a.  True
    b.  False

4.  In the news report, what reason does the Russian government give for creating this new LGBTQ law?

    a.  The law was created to counter influence from the United States.
    b.  The law was made to provide LGBTQ with more rights.
    c.  The law was crafted to improve relationships with Western countries.
    d.  The law was constructed to recreate traditional family values.

5.  According to the news report, what is the punishment for breaking the law?

    a.  Strong financial penalties
    b.  Deportation from the country
    c.  Imprisonment lasting up to one month
    d.  Imprisonment exceeding one month

6.  According to the news story, what does the new Russian law do?

    a.  It bans any mention of LGBTQ issues in the news media and print.
    b.  It bans all forms of traditional relationships on television.
    c.  It bans LGBTQ tourists or activists from entering Russia.
    d.  It bans any positive ideas of nontraditional relationships.

## 5. Creating a Summary

**Look at the options below and select A or B. Read the instructions carefully.**

**A. Writing and creating an infographic:**

Work on your writing and organizational skills by creating a poster presentation. This poster should include the main ideas of the news article written in your own words. Organize your information and data points as an infographic.

**B. Speaking and giving a presentation:**

Work on your speaking and presenting skills by creating a 2 minute pitch talk. This will be a short speech which includes a summary of the main ideas of the news article written in your own words. How can you get others to understand this news story?

## 6. Debate Exercise

**Let's discuss the topic further by having a debate. Split your class into groups and decide which group will be pro or con. The pro side will argue for the topic while the con side will argue against it.**

> Let's look at the following debate question

"Should LGBTQ laws be put into place to protect traditional values?"

**Example Con Argument**

 53

### Should LGBTQ laws be put into place to protect traditional values?

LGBTQ laws should be put into place to protect their way of life. Traditional values and marriage are important but traditions are not fixed. They often change with the times and so laws need to change as well. LGBTQ laws should be put into place to protect LGBTQ lifestyles, protect the safety of people, and promote equality between all people.

LGBTQ lifestyle should be protected. As society grows and evolves, we should always try and provide people with the freedom to be themselves. This is extremely true for consenting adults. If two people of age agree to be in a relationship, their rights should be respected.

Laws should also be made to protect the safety of people, especially in the LGBTQ community. As more LGBTQ people realize their sexual orientations, they should not be persecuted or threatened by the law. A free society must respect the freedoms for consenting adults. Any laws that are created should consider the mindset of the current age. Lawmakers must also consider people who are purposefully being targeted and used as a way to promote hate.

Finally, laws should be put into place to promote equality between all people. People who are of age, or considered adults, should be provided with equal freedoms. This means that it is not the government's job to dictate who can be with what person. Instead, adults can manage their own social relationships.

LGBTQ laws need to be created for their protection. It is easy to hate something that is different from you and it is easy to see cultures or countries that use the LGBTQ community to fan the flames of hate. Laws should be created to protect the daily lives, protection, and fairness for LGBTQ people.

**Pro teams:** Brainstorm ideas that support your argument. Include data or research to strengthen your points.

**– Countries should promote LGBTQ lifestyles...**
**– LGBTQ education should be expanded...**

**Con teams:** Brainstorm ideas that support your argument. Include data or research to strengthen your points.

– **Countries should not promote LGBTQ lifestyle…**
– **LGBTQ education should be limited…**

---

---

| Next, let's come up with our own arguments. |

**Debate Theme 2:** Is the international community doing enough to protect the rights of the LGBTQ community?

**Debate Theme 3:** Does the idea of traditional or moral values have to change in our modern society?

## 7. Mini-Research

Next, let's utilize the information we've learned so far on the topic and research some future questions about this news story. After doing some reseach, select the skills you want to practice with options A or B. Read the instructions carefully.

**A. Writing a short essay:**

Work on your writing and create a short essay (Minimum of 500 words). This short essay should include information from your research and your ideas in your own words.

**B. Speaking and giving a slide presentation:**

Work on your speaking and presentation skills by creating a 3 minute slide presentation. This slide presentation should include information from your research and your ideas in your own words.

**Review the following themes and select one to focus on:**

**Theme 1:** What countries are supportive of LGBTQ rights?

**Theme 2:** What countries are against LGBTQ rights?

**Theme 3:** Are the traditional values of countries consistent or do they differ?

**Theme 4:** Does traditional marriage and values still remain intact today?

**Theme 5:** How should the global community respond to this or future issues? For example: should they allow people to flee and seek asylum?

# 8. Project

Using all the information we have learned so far in this lesson, let's combine what we have learned and organize a final project.

**Review the following Project Prompts and select the one that interests you:**

**Project Prompt 1**  In this reading, the LGBTQ concept was used as a scapegoat for the conduct of the war. What are some concepts that have been scapegoated in warfare? Conduct research and present your findings.

**Project Prompt 2**  Why has there been limited progress in diversity inclusion in Japan? Explore potential reasons and discuss them.

---

After selecting your prompt, create your response in the form of a strong persuasive and engaging report. This report can include your thoughts in writing, data collection and analysis, as well as information from today's discussion.

---

# Fake News

## 1. Check In

Let's start our lesson by describing your experience(s) relating to our topic for today's unit.

1.  Have you ever read a news story that was not true?
2.  Where do you read news information? How do you know it is accurate?

## 2. Listening Exercise 1: Opening paragraph

**HARRAK:** Well, this election has been mired by widespread disinformation, and much of it is circulating in Spanish-speaking communities. CNN's Donie O'Sullivan shows us how these falsehoods are affecting Latino voters and their faith in democracy.

### What's next in the story?

**From the listening exercise, answer the following questions.**

1.  What do you think this news story will be about?
2.  What are some keywords you think will be important to this story?

## 3. **Listening Exercise 2:** Let's listen to the full story.

Watch the following news video and answer the questions in the next page.

1. **What is the purpose of the news story?**

   a. To discuss the impact of immigrants on elections

   b. To discuss the role of disinformation in current society and politics

   c. To highlight the importance of Latino voters in American politics

   d. To discuss the technology of apps such as Whatsapp, Instagram, and Twitter

2. **The word "disinformation" is in the news story. Which option has the closest in meaning to:**

   a. Information that is incorrect or contains mistakes

   b. Genuine information from credible sources shared to inform the public

   c. Statistics which are viewed from different perspectives

   d. Deliberately misleading information to spread to the public

3. **From the news story, why are Spanish speaking communities being targeted with disinformation?**

   a. Spanish-American communities mainly get their news from popular media outlets.

   b. Spanish-American communities are very active on Instagram to get their news.

   c. Spanish-American communities are an important vote for politicians in many areas.

   d. Spanish-American communities support socialism and want to get their message across.

## 4. Listening Exercise 3: Comprehension

Using the information you learned in the news story, select the best answer for each question.

1. According to the news report, disinformation has had a significant impact on friends and family in the Latino community.

   a. True
   b. False

2. According to the news report, Twitter is the most common platform for sharing disinformation among Latino communities.

   a. True
   b. False

3. According to the news report, socialism is a big fear in Hispanic communities.

   a. True
   b. False

4. According to the news report, why are Cuban, Venezuelan, and Nicaraguan immigrants especially targeted with disinformation?

   a. Many of these immigrants cannot speak fluent English so easily misunderstand the media.
   b. Popular news channels target these groups due to their socialist histories.
   c. These groups tend to live isolated lifestyles and are easy targets for disinformation.
   d. These groups fear Biden due to his strong handed style of leading the United States.

5. In the news story, the Spanish phrase "E que caia otoria" is used by Maria Corina Vegas. Which of these options is the closest English meaning?

   a. You should argue your ideas whenever possible.
   b. When you stay quiet, you stay out of trouble.
   c. Staying quiet allows misinformation to win.
   d. Read as much news as you can to stay informed.

6. According to the news article, why is Whatsapp the most popular app for sharing disinformation?

    a. Whatsapp has a large user base and you can share your ideas easily.

    b. Whatsapp messages allow large video or image file sizes.

    c. Whatsapp messages are encrypted and require a password to view.

    d. Whatsapp messages are encrypted and makes it difficult to fact-check.

## 5. Creating a Summary

**Look at the options below and select A or B. Read the instructions carefully.**

**A. Writing and creating an infographic:**

Work on your writing and organizational skills by creating a poster presentation. This poster should include the main ideas of the news article written in your own words. Organize your information and data points as an infographic.

**B. Speaking and giving a presentation:**

Work on your speaking and presenting skills by creating a 2 minute pitch talk. This will be a short speech which includes a summary of the main ideas of the news article written in your own words. How can you get others to understand this news story?

## 6. Debate Exercise

**Let's discuss the topic further by having a debate. Split your class into groups and decide which group will be pro or con. The pro side will argue for the topic while the con side will argue against it.**

Let's look at the following debate question

**"Is disinformation a negative thing?"**

**Example Con Argument**

# Is disinformation a negative thing?

As society grows, so does communication. This includes domestic and international relationships. As such, it exposes various news information both true and false. Disinformation is usually viewed as negative because of lies it spreads. However, disinformation can be a great way to strengthen our critical thinking, help us separate fact from fiction, and make us more cautious with the news.

Disinformation can help our critical thinking. With the internet, we are exposed to a lot of different news websites and blogs. It is important to be able to distinguish good from bad in these areas. This requires us to think carefully about who is writing this information and why.

Disinformation also helps us separate fact from fiction. As we start to recognize disinformation, we can adapt to spotting errors or areas that could be "gray" in nature. For example, some stories can be spread in different both positive and negative directions depending on the writer's intentions. The more experience we get, the more we are able to identify disinformation.

Finally, disinformation can help us be more cautious about what we believe in the future. As technology advances, so will communications and the spreading of information. Even now, new technology is being developed which is designed to trick or deceive us. It is important for us to stay educated and avoid being tricked.

Disinformation is not a negative thing. It can be positive if we use it as a tool for educating ourselves. We can improve our critical thinking and form stronger opinions. We can identify what might be true or false, and we can prepare ourselves for the future of social media.

Unit 14

**Pro teams:** Brainstorm ideas that support your argument. Include data or research to strengthen your points.

– **Disinformation is a problem because…**
– **Fact-checking is the solution to disinformation…**

**Con teams:** Brainstorm ideas that support your argument. Include data or research to strengthen your points.

– **Disinformation is not a problem because…**
– **Fact-checking is not the solution to disinformation…**

---

---

**Next, let's come up with our own arguments.**

**Debate Theme 2:** Will technology like deepfakes promote more disinformation?

**Debate Theme 3:** Should disinformation be stopped by a global organization?

## 7. Mini-Research

**Next, let's utilize the information we've learned so far on the topic and research some future questions about this news story. After doing some reseach, select the skills you want to practice with options A or B. Read the instructions carefully.**

**A. Writing a short essay:**

Work on your writing and create a short essay (Minimum of 500 words). This short essay should include information from your research and your ideas in your own words.

**B. Speaking and giving a slide presentation:**

Work on your speaking and presentation skills by creating a 3 minute slide presentation. This slide presentation should include information from your research and your ideas in your own words.

**Review the following themes and select one to focus on:**

**Theme 1:** What disinformation has been successful?

**Theme 2:** How common is it to see disinformation in social media such as WhatsApp, TikTok, Instagram, etc.?

**Theme 3:** What are some steps we can take to verify information is true or legitimate?

**Theme 4:** Why do people use disinformation? What do they gain from it?

**Theme 5:** What is the future of misinformation?

## 8. Project

**Using all the information we have learned so far in this lesson, let's combine what we have learned and organize a final project.**

**Review the following Project Prompts and select the one that interests you:**

**Project Prompt 1**     The prevalence of various types of fake news is on the rise in Japan. With the increasing sophistication of fake news and its widespread dissemination, it is becoming challenging to address each individual instance. How do you believe we should tackle this situation?

**Project Prompt 2**     Compare the unique strategies used by presidential candidates in the U.S. to engage a substantial number of citizens, which might be considered unconventional in Japan. Analyze and discuss the advantages and disadvantages of each approach in election campaigns for both Japanese and American contexts.

After selecting your prompt, create your response in the form of a strong persuasive and engaging report. This report can include your thoughts in writing, data collection and analysis, as well as information from today's discussion.

# Digital Nomads

## 1. Check In

**Let's start our lesson by describing your experience(s) relating to our topic for today's unit.**

1. What has your experience been with online work? This includes classes, homework, meetings, etc.
2. Should living in a different country require you to embrace the local culture?

## 2. Listening Exercise 1: Opening paragraph

**VAUSE:** The global (ph) pandemic forced millions to work remotely from home. But some digital nomads found it even easier to work from another country. The influx though of foreigners paying in U.S. dollars have some locals concerned about the economic impact.

CNN's David Culver has the story now from Mexico city.

### What's next in the story?

**From the listening exercise, answer the following questions.**

1. What do you think this news story will be about?
2. What are some keywords you think will be important to this story?

**3.** **Listening Exercise 2:** Let's listen to the full story. 🎧 58~60 / ▶️ 15

**Watch the following news video and answer the questions in the next page.**

1. **What is the purpose of the news story?**

    a. To discuss popular tourist sites which are trending

    b. To show how inflation is affecting prices for housing, food, etc.

    c. To illustrate a growing problem with locals and tourists

    d. To demonstrate benefits of living and working in another country

2. **The phrase "digital nomad" is used in the first paragraph. Which option has the closest meaning:**

    a. A person who enjoys the internet and exploring various websites.

    b. A person who loves to travel to new destinations and experience various cultures.

    c. A person who works from home but can also work in a cafe or restaurant.

    d. A person who works remotely and lives in another country.

3. **From the news story, why are so many Americans moving to Mexico?**

    a. To experience the local cuisine and famous attractions.

    b. To learn about Mexican culture and improve their Spanish.

    c. To use their US income to live more cheaply in Mexico.

    d. To escape the stress of the global pandemic hitting the US.

## 4. Listening Exercise 3: Comprehension

Using the information you learned in the news story, select the best answer for each question.

1. According to the news report, tourism to Mexico has increased by almost 1 million post-pandemic vs. pre-pandemic.

   a. True

   b. False

2. According to E. Rodriguez, his main motivation to move to Mexico was to find cheaper housing.

   a. True

   b. False

3. According to the news report, Mexican locals have been happy to have new people visit and live in their towns.

   a. True

   b. False

4. What is the concern with the locals and this increase in American tourism?

   a. Restaurants are seeing an increase in traffic due to more tourists.

   b. Americans have more money and can cause the prices of everyday goods to increase.

   c. Americans are not trying to embrace the local culture and many speak little if any Spanish.

   d. Many fear that they will lose their cultural identity with this increase in non-natives.

5. What is Sandra Ortiz's experience with this situation?

   a. She was kicked out and lost her business due to increasing prices in the area.

   b. She is working at a restaurant trying to make delicious meals.

   c. She is sad that she has to move but is looking forward to seeing the new accommodations.

   d. She hopes more tourists would learn more about the local culture.

6. What are the benefits for these American tourists?

   a. They can have opportunities to learn new languages.

   b. They can live a healthier lifestyle, free to exercise and work at their leisure.

   c. They can gain experience abroad which will help them improve their work.

   d. They can benefit from the currency conversion of US dollars to Mexican pesos.

## 5. Creating a Summary

Look at the options below and select A or B. Read the instructions carefully.

**A. Writing and creating an infographic:**

Work on your writing and organizational skills by creating a poster presentation. This poster should include the main ideas of the news article written in your own words. Organize your information and data points as an infographic.

**B. Speaking and giving a presentation:**

Work on your speaking and presenting skills by creating a 2 minute pitch talk. This will be a short speech which includes a summary of the main ideas of the news article written in your own words. How can you get others to understand this news story?

## 6. Debate Exercise

Let's discuss the topic further by having a debate. Split your class into groups and decide which group will be pro or con. The pro side will argue for the topic while the con side will argue against it.

Let's look at the following debate question

**"Do digital nomads have a positive effect on other countries?"**

**Example Pro Argument**

61

### Do digital nomads have a positive effect on other countries?

Digital nomads provide a great opportunity to other countries. These benefits can come in many different ways. Digital nomads can provide a stimulus to an economy, new skills which can be acquired by locals, as well as a chance for different cultures to meet and grow.

Digital nomads have a great financial impact on the countries they visit. They provide the local economies with more income and although local peoples may suffer at first, there are many ways this new money can be used by the local government to support their citizens.

Digital nomads bring with them not only income but also various skill sets. Many digital nomads work from home which makes them very familiar with technology. This leads to many opportunities for areas to learn from nomads and try and gain similar jobs and employment.

Finally, different cultures can meet and grow from each other's strong points. Digital nomads have a relatively free and open life. They can work where they like which might be a new concept for countries with a more traditional mindset. Locals also can provide valuable information to these nomads on how to accustom themselves to the new environment.

In conclusion, although it may appear to cause conflict. Digital nomads can be a great asset providing money, skills, and experience to new people. Locals will face challenges initially. There will have to be adjusting, but in the end there are many benefits to all people involved.

**Pro teams:** Brainstorm ideas that support your argument. Include data or research to strengthen your points.

– **Overall income will increase…**
– **IT skills can be learned…**

_____

_____

**Con teams:** Brainstorm ideas that support your argument. Include data or research to strengthen your points.

– **Locals will struggle to keep up financially…**
– **Tourists should not be allowed to work…**

_____

_____

## Next, let's come up with our own arguments.

**Debate Theme 2:** Digital nomads should be banned from countries.

**Debate Theme 3:** Local governments should tax digital nomads who disrupt the local citizens.

## 7. Mini-Research

Next, let's utilize the information we've learned so far on the topic and research some future questions about this news story. After doing some reseach, select the skills you want to practice with options A or B. Read the instructions carefully.

### A. Writing a short essay:

Work on your writing and create a short essay (Minimum of 500 words). This short essay should include information from your research and your ideas in your own words.

### B. Speaking and giving a slide presentation:

Work on your speaking and presentation skills by creating a 3 minute slide presentation. This slide presentation should include information from your research and your ideas in your own words.

**Review the following themes and select one to focus on:**

**Theme 1:** Are digital nomads the new normal? Is it a good thing to allow people to work wherever they please?

**Theme 2:** Should companies crack down on digital nomads and apply some penalties for "working from home" yet living abroad?

**Theme 3:** As technology improves and becomes more widespread, how can countries such as Mexico adjust to these digital nomads?

**Theme 4:** What measures can local governments take to support local businesses and avoid people like Sandra Ortiz from losing their businesses?

**Theme 5:** As mentioned in the news report, what would be the outcome if there was a culture clash?

## 8. Project

Using all the information we have learned so far in this lesson, let's combine what we have learned and organize a final project.

**Review the following Project Prompts and select the one that interests you:**

**Project Prompt 1**    What will be the future of work? Present a vision for a work model that will be commonplace in 2050.

**Project Prompt 2**    There are certain companies in Japan that offer full-remote work opportunities. Evaluate the factors behind this trend and suggest a policy that Japanese companies should adopt in the future.

---

After selecting your prompt, create your response in the form of a strong persuasive and engaging report. This report can include your thoughts in writing, data collection and analysis, as well as information from today's discussion.

---

# Canada and the Monarchy

## 1. Check In

Let's start our lesson by describing your experience(s) relating to our topic for today's unit.

1. What countries do you know have king and queens?
2. What benefits do countries get by being a group?

## 2. Listening Exercise 1: Opening paragraph

**Announcer:** Now to Canada, where the Queen Elizabeth developed close ties during her long reign. While many Canadians mourn the loss of the queen, there are also those who believe it's time for an end to the monarchy. CNN's Paula Newton shows us both sides and the challenges awaiting King Charles.

> What's next in the story?

**From the listening exercise, answer the following questions.**

1. What do you think this news story will be about?
2. What are some keywords you think will be important to this story?

**3.** **Listening Exercise 2:** Let's listen to the full story.  62~64  ▶ 16

**Watch the following news video and answer the questions in the next page.**

1. **What is the purpose of the news story?**

   a. To introduce the history of Canada and Canadian culture

   b. To discuss how the relationship with the U.K. and Canada will continue

   c. To discuss Queen Elizabeth and her history in Canada as well as with Canadian citizens

   d. To introduce how King Charles will handle future relations with Canada

2. **The phrase "testing ground" is used by Paula Newton to discuss King Charles and Canada.  Which option has the closest in meaning to:**

   a. An area for him to try to introduce new laws and legislation.

   b. A place which can become his second home like it was for Queen Elizabeth.

   c. A country which will expand its technology and social income.

   d. An area which will determine the relationship with royalty in modern times.

3. **From the news story, what challenges will King Charles face?**

   a. Canada will be a new territory for him to make negotiations with.

   b. Canada is in a state of change with people wanting to leave the royal family.

   c. Canada is suffering due to economic depression and needs financial support.

   d. Canada will have to become like a second home to King Charles.

**Listening Exercise 3:** Comprehension

Using the information you learned in the news story, select the best answer for each question.

1. According to the news report, Queen Elizabeth was very fond of Canada.

   a. True
   b. False

2. According to the news report, many Canadians felt Queen Elizabeth was like a friend living next door.

   a. True
   b. False

3. According to the news report, Canada may be the first of many countries to leave the British Commonwealth.

   a. True
   b. False

4. What reason does the news segment give for Queen Elizabeth considering Canada her second home?

   a. She was a big fan of Canadian culture and indigenous people.
   b. She was a big fan of musical performance which sparked her interest.
   c. She had close connections to the locals living in Canada.
   d. She enjoyed nature and Canada's great forests.

5. How do the indigenous people feel about the Canada and U.K. relations?

   a. They are happy their culture is respected by Queen Elizabeth.
   b. They feel the U.K. should accept responsibility for their bad history.
   c. They feel progress will be made rapidly and are looking forward to future relations.
   d. They have made some statues their top destination sites in honor of Queen Elizatbeth.

6. What challenges will King Charles find as the new King of Canada?

   a. He will be greeted with open arms by Canadians as he replaces Queen Elizabeth.
   b. He will be tested on his charm and will need to appeal to local horse events.
   c. He will need to gain the respect of indigenous people as well as charm the locals.
   d. He will need to show that Canada is his second home to appeal to other Commonwealth countries.

## 5. Creating a Summary

**Look at the options below and select A or B. Read the instructions carefully.**

### A. Writing and creating an infographic:

Work on your writing and organizational skills by creating a poster presentation. This poster should include the main ideas of the news article written in your own words. Organize your information and data points as an infographic.

### B. Speaking and giving a presentation:

Work on your speaking and presenting skills by creating a 2 minute pitch talk. This will be a short speech which includes a summary of the main ideas of the news article written in your own words. How can you get others to understand this news story?

## 6. Debate Exercise

Let's discuss the topic further by having a debate. Split your class into groups and decide which group will be pro or con. The pro side will argue for the topic while the con side will argue against it.

Let's look at the following debate question

**"Should Canada stay with the British Commonwealth or monarchy?"**

**Example Pro Argument**

 65

### Should Canada stay with the British Commonwealth or monarchy?

King Charles will face a challenge with his many responsibilities but Canada should continue their relationship with the United Kingdom. They have a long and rich history. Canada should stay with the British Commonwealth because it will continue to improve relations between countries, between people, and be part of Queen Elizabeth's legacy.

Canada staying connected with the United Kingdom will prove relations between both countries. This means more trade which will increase each country's finances. It will also increase tourism with many people wanting to visit Queen Elizabeth's "second home".

Staying connected to the United Kingdom will also improve Canadian and British relations. People who follow the same monarchy will communicate better. This extends from business to also personal.

Lastly, being a part of the United Kingdom will honor Queen Elizabeth. The queen felt Canada was like a second home so it is important for their relationship to continue in her memory. Many people in the UK mourned her loss, as did people in other commonwealth countries such as Canada and Australia.

In conclusion, Canada should stay connected with the United Kingdom and the British Commonwealth. It will improve the economies of both countries, relations between citizens, and be a true memory in honor of Queen Elizabeth.

**Pro teams:** Brainstorm ideas that support your argument. Include data or research to strengthen your points.

– **Canada should stay because...**
– **Commonwealth countries can work together to...**

_____

_____

**Con teams:** Brainstorm ideas that support your argument. Include data or research to strengthen your points.

– **Canada should leave because...**
– **Commonwealth countries cannot work together because...**

_____

_____

## Next, let's come up with our own arguments.

**Debate Theme 2:** All monarchies should be disestablished.

**Debate Theme 3:** More countries should join the commonwealth.

## 7. Mini-Research

**Next, let's utilize the information we've learned so far on the topic and research some future questions about this news story. After doing some reseach, select the skills you want to practice with options A or B. Read the instructions carefully.**

### A. Writing a short essay:

Work on your writing and create a short essay (Minimum of 500 words). This short essay should include information from your research and your ideas in your own words.

### B. Speaking and giving a slide presentation:

Work on your speaking and presentation skills by creating a 3 minute slide presentation. This slide presentation should include information from your research and your ideas in your own words.

**Review the following themes and select one to focus on:**

**Theme 1:** What are the benefits of a monarchy?

**Theme 2:** What are the demerits of a monarchy?

**Theme 3:** As the world gets more globalized, is it important to keep relations such as Canada and the United Kingdom?

**Theme 4:** As the world gets more globalized, is it important for countries like Canada to become independent?

**Theme 5:** What do you think the future will be for the British monarchy?

## 8. Project

**Using all the information we have learned so far in this lesson, let's combine what we have learned and organize a final project.**

**Review the following Project Prompts and select the one that interests you:**

**Project Prompt 1**   Barbados has abolished the British monarchy and established itself as a republic. Let's speculate on the future of the British monarchy and its relationship with the Commonwealth.

**Project Prompt 2**   Charles III made an unusual attempt by inviting kings from other countries to his coronation. What kind of new approach do you think the Japanese public would like to see from their emperors?

After selecting your prompt, create your response in the form of a strong persuasive and engaging report. This report can include your thoughts in writing, data collection and analysis, as well as information from today's discussion.

## CNN News English: Engaging College Students as Active Learners

検印
省略

©2024 年 1 月 31 日　第 1 版発行

編著者　　　　　　　山　中　　司
　　　　　　　　　　Rafael Roman
　　　　　　　　　　豊　島　　知　穂

発行者　　　　　　　小　川　　洋一郎
発行所　　　　　　　株式会社 朝 日 出 版 社
　　　　　　　〒101-0065 東京都千代田区西神田 3-3-5
　　　　　　　　　　電話　東京　(03) 3239-0271
　　　　　　　　　　FAX　東京　(03) 3239-0479
　　　　　　　E-mail　text-e@asahipress.com
　　　　　　　　　　振替口座　00140-2-46008
　　　　　　　　　　http://www.asahipress.com/
　　　　　　　組版／メディアアート　製版／図書印刷

ISBN 978-4-255-15715-3